For Jim —
regards,
Dick
8/4/92

GRAHAM GREENE

A Study of the Short Fiction

Also available in Twayne's Studies in Short Fiction Series

Twayne's Studies in Short Fiction

Gordon Weaver, General Editor
Oklahoma State University

GRAHAM GREENE
By permission of Personality Photos, Inc.

GRAHAM GREENE

A Study of the Short Fiction

Richard Kelly

TWAYNE PUBLISHERS • NEW YORK
Maxwell Macmillan Canada • Toronto
Maxwell Macmillan International • New York Oxford Singapore Sydney

Twayne's Studies in Short Fiction Series, No. 35

Copyright © 1992 by Twayne Publishers

Twayne Publishers
Macmillan Publishing Company
866 Third Avenue
New York, New York 10022

Maxwell Macmillan Canada, Inc.
1200 Eglinton Avenue East
Suite 200
Don Mills, Ontario M3C 3N1

Macmillan Publishing Company is part of the Maxwell Communication Group of Companies

Library of Congress Cataloging-in-Publication Data

Kelly, Richard Michael, 1937–
    Graham Greene : a study of the short fiction / Richard Kelly.
        p.   cm.—(Twayne's studies in short fiction ; no. 35)
    Includes bibliographical references and index.
    ISBN 0-8057-8342-3 : $40.00
    1. Greene, Graham, 1904–   —Criticism and interpretation.
    2. Short story. I. Title. II. Series.
    PR6013.R44Z6346   1992
    823'.912—dc20   91-45633
                                                                      CIP

10 9 8 7 6 5 4 3 2 1

Printed in the United States of America

In memory of Mary Russell

Contents

Preface

In a prefatory note to his first collection of short stories, *Nineteen Stories* (1947), Graham Greene disparagingly refers to his tales as merely the "by-products of a novelist's career."[1] Twenty-five years later, in the introduction to his *Collected Stories*, he revises his estimate of those and subsequent stories by declaring he was "misled," that "since the beginning I have really been all the time a writer of short-stories—they are not the 'scraps' I thought them."[2] Nevertheless, he goes on to declare himself "a novelist who has happened to write short stories, just as there are certain short story writers . . . who have happened to write novels" (*CS*, vii). As a novelist he views the short story as "a form of escape—escape from having to live with another character for years on end, picking up his jealousies, his meanness, his dishonest tricks of thought, his betrayals" (*CS*, ix). In summary, he suggests all of his short stories "can be regarded as a collection of escapes from the novelist's world—even, if you like, of escapades" (*CS*, x).

Over the years Greene has enjoyed the opportunity of categorizing his works as a means of fending off his critics. Between 1932 and 1958 he published seven novels he labeled "entertainments." He viewed these works as melodramas or thrillers, with the emphasis upon action rather than character. Sometimes he played with his labels, as when he moved *Brighton Rock* from the category of entertainment to that of novel. He dissolved the distinction between these two groups in 1969 with the publication of the comic novel *Travels with My Aunt*, a work that earlier he clearly would have grouped with his entertainments. Many critics today ignore Greene's distinction between novels and entertainments, as do his publishers, who now list all of his long fiction under the heading of novels.

There is a parallel between Greene's labeling some of his early novels "entertainments" and his early short stories "scraps." In both cases he attempts to protect himself from critical attack by suggesting that he does not take these works seriously, a stance belied by their publication throughout England and the United States. In the 1970s, by which time he had acquired an international reputation as one of the foremost authors of his day, he revised his earlier defensive labels and declared the entertainments novels and the scraps short stories.

If the critical response during the past four decades to Greene's works is any indication, then his view of himself as a novelist who happens to write short stories is indeed justified. The great outpouring of books and articles about him focuses almost exclusively upon his novels. In addition, there have been a few recent studies of the films based upon his novels. One has to look far and wide, however, to discover any critical assessment of his short stories. The few essays that do discuss his work in that genre appeared years ago.

Greene's future reputation will clearly be based upon the quality of his many novels. His film criticism, literary essays, dramas, travel books, and short stories will continue to be overshadowed by his achievement as a novelist. Nevertheless, his work in all those genres is deserving of more critical attention than it has received. Indeed, some of his short stories possess a greater degree of purity in their simplicity and theme than do several of his novels. The following analysis of his short stories, combined with selected critical essays about them and Greene's own commentary upon his writing, attempts to demonstrate the achievement of Graham Greene as a notable author of short fiction.

In order to lay the groundwork for understanding Greene's development as a writer of short fiction, I shall begin this study with an examination of the uncollected stories he published during his student years at Berkhamsted and Oxford, during the period 1921–25. Continuing in chronological order, I shall use the *Collected Stories* as the basis for most of my study. I do this for two reasons: first, because Greene views this collection as the one that represents his best work in the genre; and second, because this volume is readily accessible in most libraries. There are, however, some peculiarities to be noted about *Collected Stories*: it reproduces the three previous collections in reverse chronological order and also alters the arrangement of some of the stories originally published in *Twenty-One Stories*. Furthermore, it adds three previously uncollected stories to the section containing *A Sense of Reality*. In order to maintain a feel for Greene's development as a writer of short fiction I shall ignore the peculiar arrangement of *Collected Stories* and discuss the three sections ("Twenty-One Stories," "A Sense of Reality," and "May We Borrow Your Husband?") and the stories within them in chronological order.

The Last Word, published in 1990, contains a surprising mix of previously uncollected stories. Five of the stories originally appeared between 1923 and 1940, two in the 1950s, four in the 1980s, and one is published for the first time. Since this volume apparently represents Greene's "last word" as a writer of short fiction, I shall discuss the stories chronologically in order to reflect the synoptic view of his life that Greene achieves in this collection.

Finally, in the chapter entitled Misbegotten Tales, I shall examine five stories Greene excluded from his canon. These include the experimental *The Bear Fell Free*, published in book form in 1935, "The Other Side of the Border" (which originally appeared in *Nineteen Stories* but which was never subsequently collected), "Voyage in the Dark" (1938), "The Escapist" (1939), and "All But Empty" (1947).

Notes

1. "Author's Note," *Nineteen Stories* (London: Heinemann, 1947), vii.

2. "Introduction," *Collected Stories* (London: Bodley Head/William Heinemann, 1972), vii; hereafter cited in text as *CS*.

Acknowledgments

Excerpts from Marie-Françoise Allain's *The Other Man: Conversations with Graham Greene* are reprinted by permission of the Bodley Head. Copyright © 1983 by the Bodley Head, Ltd.

Gwen R. Boardman's "Greene's 'Under the Garden': Aesthetic Explorations" is reprinted by permission of *Renascence* from *Renascence* 17 (Summer 1965): 180–90, 194.

A. R. Coulthard's "Graham Greene's 'The Hint of an Explanation': A Reinterpretation" is reprinted by permission of Newberry College from *Studies in Short Fiction* 8 (Fall 1971): 601–5.

Graham Greene's "Introduction" to *Collected Stories* is reprinted by permission of Viking Penguin, a division of Penguin Books USA, Inc., and by permission of William Heinemann, Ltd. and the Bodley Head, Ltd. Copyright (c) 1972 by Graham Greene. All rights reserved.

John Ower's "Dark Parable: History and Theology in Graham Greene's 'The Destructors'" is reprinted by permission of *Cithara* from *Cithara* 15 (Nov. 1975): 69–78.

Excerpts from *Why Do I Write?*, published by Percival Marshall in 1948, are reprinted by permission of William Heinemann, Ltd. and the Bodley Head, Ltd.

Frontispiece photograph used by permission of Personality Photos, Inc.

Part 1

THE SHORT FICTION

Loosing the Devils

Rarely has a writer been more obsessed with his lost childhood than has Graham Greene. In this respect he is clearly the child of the romantic period, whose poets, such as Blake and Wordsworth, celebrate the bright joys of innocence that quickly give way to the dark pains of experience. Greene also found his obsession mirrored in the novels of Charles Dickens, where Victorian society seems dead set upon destroying the bodies and souls of children. Similarly, Greene's admiration for the minor Victorian poet Arthur Hugh Clough, whom he calls the only adult poet of the age, derives from his own spiritual malaise. During Clough's years at Oxford he lost the serenity of his Christian faith and turned to writing poetry as a means of defending himself against the doubts that raged against his desire for belief in God. Like Clough, Greene's sense of dislocation from his childhood and from his Christian faith intensified during his Oxford days, and he sought to overcome his depression and to exorcise his psychic demons through his writing.

As a highly sensitive, imaginative youth, and coming from a respected, comfortable, upper-middle-class family, Greene enjoyed the opportunity to develop more exotic emotional problems than are allotted to children of the lower classes. When he first discovered that he could read, he hid this fact from his parents out of fear that they would make him enter preparatory school. He began to live a covert life, secretly reading books about adventure and mystery that his parents would not approve. As a child he also developed inordinate fears of the dark, of birds and bats, of drowning, and of the footsteps of strangers. He developed recurrent nightmares about a witch who would lurk at night near the linen cupboard in the nursery.

As a student at Berkhamsted School, where his father was headmaster, Greene's emotional problems were compounded by his sense of divided loyalties. His filial devotion was constantly challenged by his desire to be one of the boys. He was never able to resolve these conflicting loyalties, and, to make matters worse, two schoolboys, named Carter and Wheeler, sadistically exploited Greene's anxiety with cruel psychological precision. Greene has not disclosed specific

3

details of their torment, but Norman Sherry, in his biography of Greene, has shown that these two boys, especially Carter, exercised a powerful control over Greene during a critical time in his development. More experienced in worldly matters, they took pleasure in attacking Greene's naïveté and trust. Lionel Carter not only tormented Greene for being the headmaster's son, but, after winning his confidence and discovering his secret dreams and desires, he disabused Greene of many of his romantic and chivalric ideals. As the murderer of Greene's childhood and as the arch-betrayer, Carter would appear in many guises throughout Greene's stories and novels and become one of the powerful demons Greene would spend his life as a writer attempting to exorcise. Years later Greene was to observe, "Every creative writer worth our consideration . . . is a victim: a man given over to an obsession."[1]

In 1920 Greene's manic-depressive and suicidal behavior led his parents to send him to a psychoanalyst named Kenneth Richmond for treatment. The experience proved beneficial and Greene began self-consciously to record and analyze his dreams and feelings. It was also during this period that he began to write short stories, which served, perhaps unwittingly, to shape and help control his inchoate fears and depressions.

The short stories Greene began writing then and later during his years at Berkhamsted School and Oxford University have been largely ignored by critics and scholars, and yet they are fundamental to an understanding of his character and his development as a writer. Uncollected and not easily accessible, these stories, written during the period 1920–25, reveal the youthful obsessions that were to inform all his later work. It seems important, therefore, to examine these early creations for what they reveal about Greene the man and the writer, for, as Wordsworth says, "The child is father of the man."

Several of Greene's juvenilia, being only a page or two in length, fail to develop character, plot, or scene; rather, they sketch a mood, fear, or anxiety, usually in a self-conscious literary or allegorical form. "The Tick of the Clock," for example, which was published in Greene's school magazine, the *Berkhamstedian*, in 1920, when he was only 16 years old, reveals his youthful morbidity. The story is about a lonely old lady facing death with no companion but her ticking clock. Her only wish in life was to love someone, but young men had never come her way and children now fear her. The clock attempts to console her by relating the fate of a king and a poet who unhappily died with an

4

uneasy conscience and a failed sense of glory: "But you, you have no sin upon your conscience, you have not sought for fame or wealth, why then do you find death so hard?"[2] When the woman replies that she cannot face death "without Love to hold me up," Fate speaks to her in Christ-like tones: "O woman of little understanding, wherefore are you sad? Do you not know that I am Fate and Fate is Death, and Death is Love Eternal? Your quest is ended, you have found that which you sought" ("Tick," 119). The next morning she is discovered dead in her bed and those who see her exclaim, "How happy she looks" ("Tick," 119).

The heavy-handed allegory, the melodrama, and the unconvincing consolation offered to the old woman by Fate all mark this story as a youthful exercise. Beneath the literary posturing, however, one can detect the young Greene's concern about his own rather loveless life and the void that enhances its misery. Greene's romantic assertion that death is eternal love is a bit like whistling in the dark. It is an idea belied by his later work in which his expiring heroes and heroines are sent to anxious and uncertain fates.

In his autobiography, *A Sort of Life* (1971), Greene looks back upon "The Tick of the Clock" with mixed emotions. He abhors the story as literature but recalls its publication—his first—as inspiring him with confidence and a sense of glory:

> I was beginning to write the most sentimental fantasies in bad poetic prose. One abominable one, called "The Tick of the Clock," about an old woman's solitary death, was published in the school magazine. I cut out the pages and posted them to the *Star*, an evening paper of the period, and for God knows what reason they published the story and sent me a check for three guineas. I took the editor's kindly letter and the complimentary copy up to the Commons and for hours I sat on the abandoned rifle butts reading the piece aloud to myself. . . . Now, I told myself, I was really a professional writer, and never again did the idea hold such excitement, pride and confidence. . . . that sunny afternoon I could detect no flaw in "The Tick of the Clock." The sense of glory touched me for the first and last time.[3]

In "The Poetry of Modern Life," published in the *Berkhamstedian* in 1921, Greene implicitly acknowledges Carter's disturbing effect upon his ideals. The narrator of the story is overwhelmed by a voice that declares the death of poetry in modern life: "It was just a voice in the street that I heard as I passed along, 'Poetry and Romance are dead' . . . when I heard that voice, the busy movement of the streets pressed in upon me, seeming to shut out all colour, and changing everything into a dull monotony . . . it even penetrated into my slumbers so that I seemed to be surrounded with legions of devils, all crying out, 'Poetry and Romance are dead.'"[4] In a desperate attempt to deal with his painful disillusionment, the narrator reverts to the literary past and seeks counsel from a chivalric knight. The knight, however, merely confesses that he and his kind are dead and offers the narrator the weak consolation that there is heroic virtue in the poetry of defeat: "As long as heroic deeds are done, as long as the great world struggle between Good and Evil lasts, so long will there be poetry in life. . . . Ye know the poetry of victory, the wild enthusiasm of a people when long looked for peace arrives. But have ye yet learned the poetry of defeat?" ("Modern Life," 4). The story concludes with this theme by describing three men dying of hunger and cold, "yet one was still striving to write some last letters to those at home, thinking in his last moments, not of himself, but of the man who had sent him and trying to save him from vain, useless regret" ("Modern Life," 4).

Norman Sherry suggests that Greene might have been thinking of the deaths of Captain Scott and his associates Wilson and Bowers in the Antarctic, since Scott's dramatic death in the Antarctic in 1912 made him a great hero among English schoolboys. More significantly, however, Sherry connects this story by Greene with his persecution by Carter:

> Perhaps the dying man's attempt to write letters home reflects Graham's desire to write to his parents about his misery, though he could not. In the face of Carter's undermining of Greene's cherished boyhood beliefs, it is not surprising that he turned to a less romantic vision. The knight in the story offers some hope, arguing that "as long as the great world struggle between Good and Evil lasts, so long will there be poetry in life." It is possible that Carter, with his inexplicable cruelties, his nihilism, his ability to feign innocence, put Greene on to his fundamental theme, the nature of Good and Evil and the conflict between them.[5]

In another story, "Castles in the Air" (1921), which earned him a first prize in a school competition, Greene reverts to the subject of disillusionment and death, heralded again by his personal devil, Lionel Carter. During the festivities at the Great Grinsted's Midsummer Fair, a grotesque piper begins to play strange music that brings an end to the noisy pleasures of the crowd and makes everyone aware of his mortal sadness. Greene's memorable description of the piper anticipates the grotesque character of the mestizo, another betrayer, in *The Power and the Glory*: "a short, hunched man, one-eyed, covered in dirt, with a great red bulbous nose protruding aggressively from his face. . . . The man grinned, disclosing great, dirty, fang-like teeth."[6]

As the piper plays, his music conjures up in the minds of the crowd visions of beauty and romance: "to each onlooker he was different. To some he seemed a princess, with beautiful braided hair, to others as a glorious knight in shining coat of mail, but to all he was their childhood's dream of love. He was the mistress, he was the lord of those lovely twisted white marble palaces which all had constructed once, stone upon stone, in the clouds" ("Castles," 113). The piper's seductive tune offers intimations of childhood immortality for all of his listeners, but then he disappears and the crowd is left in dismal silence "each with his private grief" ("Castles," 113). The devil incarnate, the piper steals the very dreams of childhood love and romance he conjured up in the imaginations of his listeners.

Greene believed that his personal tormenter, Lionel Carter, destroyed his childhood joy and dreams. It is interesting to note that Greene presents the devil as a piper. The legendary piper plays music that is both seductive and destructive, thereby suggesting that Carter's imposition of his adult view of life upon Greene's youthful fantasies combines both alluring and terrifying prospects.

While he was under the psychiatric care of Kenneth Richmond, Greene wrote a story entitled "The Creation of Beauty: A Study in Sublimation." Unlike the other early tales, with their emphasis upon mortality and disillusionment, this one lives up to its subtitle by offering a defense against fear and unhappiness through the escapist ideal of feminine beauty. Greene's repressed sexuality—during his teens he was infatuated with several women, including a ballet student who used to visit the Richmonds—thus finds an outlet in this story about cosmic creation.

The chief architect of the universe confronts God with his misery. Following God's orders he had created man and the universe but now he is distressed that God gave man no other happiness than a woman to love. Furthermore, God has ordered the existence of darkness and sleep, which contain fear and evil dreams to torment man. All of nature, in fact, seems to conspire to harm man and defeat his work and his dreams. God answers that "because you have given him the beauty of woman, you have given him the beauty of the universe."[7] God declares that good and evil are reconciled in man's devotion to woman:

> He will love the cold, because it is like his wayward mistress; he will love the heat, because it is as warm as her breast. He will write songs to the dark, because it is as deep, unfathomable and mysterious as love, and drowns him in the blackness of her hair. He will let himself down into sleep with a fear, because, though it bring evil dreams, yet will it also bring dreams of her for whom he lives. He will glory in the birds, for he will decorate her in their feathers. (Sherry 1989–, 1:101)

In the midst of this lyrical celebration, Greene attributes to his femme fatale the power to assuage and reconcile many of his most profound fears: of sexuality, of the dark, of bad dreams, of drowning, and of birds. The story reads almost like a psychoanalytical exercise whereby through the sublimation of his fears into a cosmic hymn to female beauty and through the act of writing itself Greene may obtain a sense of control over his demons. Like his character God, Greene can assume the role of creator through his fiction, imposing order upon the chaos of his experience and illuminating the dark corners of his fears.

The two stories Greene published in 1922, "The Tyranny of Realism" and "Magic," extend some of the former themes and reveal his continuing sexual repression, guilt, desire for punishment, and sense of betrayal and disappointment. Roland Wobbe was the first to note the significance of "The Tyranny of Realism." He sees it as a self-conscious and paradigmatic dream story important to an understanding of Greene's later work: "The story's characters reappear in a number of later variations, and its plot becomes a schematic for the conflicts in the later novels and entertainments."[8]

"The Tyranny of Realism," published in the *Berkhamstedian* in 1922, is an allegorical fantasy that focuses upon a young boy held captive by an omnipotent tyrant named King Realism, "from whom no secrets were hid, no dark places safe."[9] Sharing the boy's captivity and lying at the King's feet in a cold marble hall filled with the smell of a prison, corruption, and repression, is a beautiful maiden called Fantasie. The boy asks the King why his great love, Fantasie, has been stolen from him and complains that he has been robbed of his dreams and of a mystical homeland of dark caves and hidden ways, full of beauty and sweet fears. King Realism informs the boy that he is no longer imprisoned and the small room melts into rolling plains and a star-filled sky. When the boy kneels before him he discovers that the King has become God and on the throne next to him sits Fantasie, "and their lips were pressed each to each in a long passion of joy" ("Tyranny," 3).

Wobbe's interpretation of this final scene lays the biographical framework for understanding the story:

> The final action leaves no doubt that both the God-king and the girl have betrayed the boy, and the allegorical significance of the characters begins to crystallize. The maid stands for fancy, romance, the erotic and a certain ambivalence; the God-king represents a changeable (perhaps arbitrary) authority, discipline, repression, cold, puritanical objectivity and male competition. One easily identifies the boy prisoner as the depressed young writer who feels both captive and spy in his father's school. The story contains heavy Freudian associations of repressed sexuality, guilt, and punishment (2).

King Realism seems to be a composite of Lionel Carter and Greene's father. Both of these figures served to undermine Greene's sense of freedom, spontaneity, and fantasy. They both exercised authority over him and demanded his loyalty. Greene's youthful dreams and chivalric eroticism, embodied in the character of Fantasie, are destroyed by the father-bully. The boy asks King Realism, "Why did you send that cold, peering slave, that Spiritualism there, to drive away my dreams, the ghosts, who used to kiss my lips and hair?" ("Tyranny," 3). The question elucidates the psychological allegory. Berkhamsted School is the prison ruled by Mr. Greene (King Realism) and the students are the slaves "who lined the walls" ("Tyranny," 2). Greene's father is then held responsible for destroying Greene's romantic idealism by his authoritarian rule and especially by imprisoning him with Carter, "the cold, peering slave" ("Tyranny," 3).

The boy's release from his imprisonment turns out to be the cruelest irony, for he has been released into the larger world of adult experience where betrayal can now be recognized and innocence lamented. The boy's discovery of King Realism in an impassioned embrace with Fantasie suggests his painful role in the oedipal triangle. Greene later modifies this oedipal relationship in "The Basement Room," where he has Philip discover Baines and Emmy together in a restaurant. In that story Baines is the figure associated with fantasy who betrays the boy's innocence.

Greene's next story, "Magic," published in the *Weekly Westminster Gazette* six weeks after the appearance of "The Tyranny of Realism," is another dream story. A writer of children's fairy stories is haunted by the spirits of children who have read his books and who are now imprisoned within his fictional fairylands. These child ghosts express their various disillusionments: one has discovered that his mythical princess is actually an old woman who wears a corset and paints her face; another has found that the king's daughter, for whom he slew dragons, first ignores him and later runs off with someone else; and a king's daughter exclaims that the young man who rescued her from a dragon turned out to be an abusive, alcoholic husband who eats his peas with a knife.

While most of the ghostly readers bitterly complain of their disillusionment with the romantic view of life the author had instilled in them as children, one of them announces his loss of religious belief as well: "I entered the gardens of heaven to fight with the archangels, and there was nothing there save weed-grown paths. I entered the halls of God, and there was only an empty throne."[10]

Finally, the author asks if he has given happiness to anyone and he is answered by the ghost of his own youth: "You showed me the door to happiness and I went in, and faeryland was more beautiful than any dream of yours. I went in, but they pulled me out and closed the door, and for me also there was nothing left" ("Magic," 16). This young spirit, unlike the other speakers, goes on to rationalize his disillusionment be arguing that the intensity of love and beauty in fairyland is too powerful for mere mortals and that one had best settle for a life of more ordinary happiness. "Love there was like a beacon fire," he says, "here like a smouldering hearth. Yet we may warm ourselves at that hearth for a little while, you and I, and perhaps forget the beacon. It is safer so. It might have scorched us" ("Magic," 16).

Besides battling his personal school dragons once again in this story, Greene is gradually discovering the subject matter and central themes of his future fiction. His overpowering sense of fantasy, which he nourished during the covert period of his childhood by reading such books as Rider Haggard's *King Solomon's Mines*, Charlotte Yonge's *The Little Duke*, Captain Frederick Marryat's *The Children of the Forest*, the fairy stories of Andrew Lang, and the tales of Beatrix Potter, must now be counterpointed by his profound disillusionment embodied within a fiction that accommodates cruel and brutal realities. It is little wonder, then, that a novelist such as Joseph Conrad would emerge as Greene's literary hero, a man who takes the dreams and illusions of a character like Charles Marlow, in *The Heart of Darkness*, and crushes them against the savage cruelty of a figure like Mr. Kurtz.

By the time he began his studies at Oxford University, Greene had all but lost any belief in God. His undergraduate atheism derived from several causes: his psychoanalysis under Kenneth Richmond, which hastened his disillusionment with the Protestant church; his rebellion against the unquestioning faith of his parents; and the opportunity afforded him at Oxford to explore new intellectual ideas and to challenge conventional principles.

In his first story for the *Oxford Outlook*, called "The Trial of Pan" (1923), Greene attempts to shock the traditional members of Balliol College by describing the seductive charms of a pagan who liberates God's followers from his stern, tyrannical rule. Greene here has at least two literary antecedents: Shelley, who, as an undergraduate at Oxford proclaiming the necessity of atheism, relished his Promethean role in attacking symbols and figures of authority, and Swinburne who, in his early poetry, asserted the superiority of the free and lustful pagan gods over the repressive and puritanical God of Christianity.

Greene's story opens on a light satirical note and establishes a tone characteristic of his later comical work in *May We Borrow Your Husband?*. God, in the company of his angels and his worthies, is busily judging the souls of prostitutes, murderers, robbers, and swindlers. The story then moves to Gabriel's defense of Lady Hope-Smithies against the charges that she boxed the ears of an Anglican curate, lost money playing bridge, and gave money to a cousin. Michael, however, demolishes the defense, accusing the defendant of always reciting "Little Annie's Deathbed" at village concerts and of keeping six pet dogs. "God summed up against her, and the jury pronounced her guilty, without leaving the box."[11]

Greene then modulates the tone of the story to one of heavy melodrama as Pan comes before God for judgment. Greene contrasts the youthful, sexual, and energetic character of Pan with the old, gloomy, and lifeless figure of God. Asked to defend himself before judgment is passed, Pan announces that he can best express himself through his music. His sensual melodies soon capture the minds and hearts of all the inhabitants of Heaven: "Never before in all Eternity had such a tune been heard in the realms of Heaven. There was not a sound in the room. The jury, the counsels, all leaned forward in a dream. And the light in their eyes changed with the changing music" ("Pan," 49).

God, however, reveals himself to be out of touch with the dreams and desires of his people. He laughs at the momentary power of Pan's music and laughs at the idea of sensual pleasures set against the joys of Heaven: the cross, the sacred music, the purity, love, and peace. But as Pan's music continues to seduce the heavenly host back to a dark, primitive world of sexual pleasure and youthful freedom, God begins to feel old and weak: "He put his hand to his head. It was aching and he was feeling old. He felt that if the music went on much longer he would weep. There was something wrong with his nerves to-day" ("Pan," 50). When the music finally ceases God realizes everyone has deserted him to follow Pan. The story ends with a description of an old, saddened, betrayed God sitting alone in the empty hall playing ticktacktoe with himself on his blotting pad.

The tale is essentially an allegory of Greene's rite of passage in which he overthrows the restrictive authority of his religious father in order to assert his sexual identity. The only segments of this heavy-handed story that point to Greene's later style are the brief satiric account of the judgment of Lady Hope-Smithies and the description of a decrepit God attempting to recall the dim past: "It was such a long, long time since he had made the world. After all, one couldn't remember everything, and it had turned out very nicely. But still he wished he could remember why he had done it all. It might be important" ("Pan," 50). No other Oxford undergraduate could have written these sentences.

"The Improbable Tale of the Archbishop of Canterbridge," published in the *Cherwell* in 1924, adds a few interesting twists to Greene's atheism. The Archbishop of Canterbridge solemnly announces to a small gathering of his peers that England and the world are doomed:

> Our cause in England, the cause of Peace and the cause of Christ, is defeated; England is doomed, she has doomed herself. A lunatic has led her dancing to dabble her feet in blood, and the notes of his mad pipings have begun to penetrate even to Europe. Gentlemen, in a month's time the world will be fighting like a pack of mad dogs. The madman with his talk of the joys of war has bewitched mankind. If it were not that this is the twentieth century I should call him Satan.[12]

The Archbishop tells his associates he will go to the home of this incarnate devil and murder him while he is taking a bath. "I realize," he says, "that I am risking my own soul, by meeting blood with blood. But, as I have said, I do it for the good of the world" ("Improbable Tale," 189).

Despite the allegorical nature of the story, the final scene is presented in graphically realistic terms that anticipate the style of Greene's later stories. After the Archbishop fires a shot he sees his victim cough up a stream of blood: "He lay still for a moment in the blood-stained water, with his head, white with soap, resting on the brass taps" ("Improbable Tale," 191).

Greene then reverts to an allegorical conversation between the representative of the Church of England (Canterbridge for Canterbury) and evil incarnate. After expressing his fear that by taking justice into his own hands he might have damned his soul, the Archbishop receives a stunning revelation from his victim: "You will find no God. . . . I am God" ("Improbable Tale," 191). The Archbishop asks him how he can be dying if he is God, and the story closes with the bleeding man's response: "'I made myself man,' murmured he who was once God, and sleep crept into his tones. "A miracle . . . Very rash . . . I have done better in my day.' They were a child's eyes that twinkled up from between the H and C taps. 'Such miracles I've done. You wouldn't believe. Woods, and wars, and sheep paths, and—and you, my dear Canterbridge.' And in a bubble of bloodstained laughter God died" ("Improbable Tale," 191).

Despite its melodrama, bizarre theology, and allegorical characters, this story marks a significant development in Greene's thinking about the nature of good and evil. He now portrays God and Satan as one and the same. Like Dr. Jekyll and Mr. Hyde, the creator and the destroyer are paradoxically incarnate as one in the mortal body of man. The story self-consciously allegorizes Greene's own manic-depressive personality.

Long after he became a convert to Catholicism, he continued to develop this paradoxical theme through such characters as Trevor in "The Destructors," Pinkie Brown in *Brighton Rock*, and Raven in *A Gun for Sale*. All three characters possess a childlike innocence and yet they all are dangerously destructive. Greene's theology is largely conditioned by his sense of a ravished childhood, thereby leading him to portray evil in rich, palpable detail that blocks out any light from the City of God. Greene's most compelling image of paradise is not based

on orthodox Christian theology but instead represents his own Eden
of dreamy innocence. Expelled from the Garden of Berkhamsted,
Greene seeks God in the past, in the myth of his lost childhood, and
not in some future paradise. The world once was bright and good, he
seems to argue, but now is brutal and evil. Therefore God is Satan, the
creator and the destroyer, who made the sheep paths and woods to
frame humanity's innocence and then trampled it with wars and
murders.

Two final stories from Greene's Oxford years, "The New House,"
published in the *Oxford Outlook* in 1923, and "The Lord Knows," published in the *Oxford Chronicle* in 1925, show him moving into his stride
as a more restrained writer, abandoning heavy-handed symbolism,
allegory, and fantasy for a down-to-earth dramatization of the clash
between dreams and reality.

"The New House" deals with a middle-aged architect named
Handry, who has long harbored a dream of designing and building a
house that would harmonize with a particular tract of land. Josephs, the
wealthy owner of the land, grants the architect a commission to
develop the tract and build the house, but Handry soon discovers his
aesthetic dream house is not what his client desires—he wants a
structure that will symbolize his wealth and power, a landmark that can
be seen for miles.

The conflict between dream and reality, beauty and power, overwhelms Handry and he leaves his meeting with Josephs and "dashed
into the road as if from an evil spell, and yet he knew that all this
struggle was in vain. He was trapped, held fast by the ropes that bind
all, his wife, his family, the world. Soon he would come slinking back,
mouthing embarrassing apologies, to perpetrate the betrayal."[13]

In the denouement, years after the building is completed, two
passersby comment on the monstrosity: "This used to be one of the
most beautiful views in the country. That fellow Joseph's [sic] philan-
thropy goes too far. His architect was a fellow in the village here, with
no more views on art than the average rustic. And the abomination is
a waste, for Josephs never lives in it, never comes near it" ("New
House," 115).

Handry, now an old man "with pathetic, puzzled eyes," who
happens to be standing near the two passersby, reveals his corruption
as he echoes the values and language of his former employer: "It is so
imposing, and such a landmark. It can be seen for miles. . . . Once
I disliked it, but I had queer ideas in those days. . . . Do you read

Longfellow? You should. He has very inspiring ideas" ("New House," 115).

As Roland Wobbe points out, "In this story Greene brings the power of his 'devils' down to earth, as the power of wealth is equated with the economic pressure of the whole society" (4). Throughout his life Greene retained the romantic notion that capitalism is the Satanic enemy of integrity, creativity, and art. Greene resurrects the prototype of Josephs for the character of Eric Krogh, an industrialist with dwarfed aesthetic tastes, in *England Made Me* (1935) and for the Satanic capitalist Doctor Fischer in *Doctor Fischer of Geneva or the Bomb Party* (1980).

"The Lord Knows," published in the *Oxford Chronicle* in 1925, is another tale of disillusionment. A young man who is about to get married enters a local pub to celebrate his future happiness. He is soon set upon by the local cynic and a drunk, both of whom poke fun at his sexual innocence and suggest his fiancée may not be a virgin. To make his point, the drunk lures a spider to his finger, which he has dipped into his whisky. The young man's celebration is ruined. The romance of marriage has been undermined by brutal jokes and disturbing sexual questions.

The touch of genius in this tale lies in Greene's depiction of the drunk's seduction of the spider. As the young man is discussing his forthcoming marriage with the bartender and the cynic, the drunk in the background continues to attend to the spider until he possesses it: "Off its thin scaffolding in the roof stepped delicately a spider. It swayed slowly down through space, undisturbed by the two high voices. It was very deliberate."[14] At that moment the young man cries out in a childish voice for the men to stop spoiling things, walks out of the pub, and exclaims, "Anyway, I've won her." The drunk, however, now holds the large spider in his hand and says, "She's come, I knew she'd come; I've won her" ("Lord Knows," 16).

In reading "The Lord Knows," one is again reminded of Carter's battering of Greene's dreams of chivalric romance. While at Berkhamsted Greene used to go off by himself to read the romantic poetry of Lewis Norris, whose *Epic of Hades* celebrates the loves of Helen and Cleopatra. Norman Sherry speculates that Greene may have confided his secret erotic dreams to Wheeler in the first flush of their friendship and that later Wheeler betrayed Greene by reporting the details to Carter, who cynically used them to ridicule and humiliate Greene (1:161).

As beneficial as it may have been for Greene to work out his terrors and frustrations through the psychodrama of his early fiction, most of the stories, because of their crude symbolism and abstractions, fail to connect with the experience of his readers. But Greene was learning that his personal devils might be recognized by others if they were presented in the guise of crass capitalists, cynics, and foolish drunks rather than as allegorical figures. In the future he would embody these devils in such forms as cruel policemen, greedy smugglers, untrustworthy mestizos, pious priests, and foreign dictators. As Greene matured and began traveling about the world, he discovered his personal demons had taken up residence everywhere, from Haiti to Indochina.

Ultimately, however, Greene's early stories serve only as a temporary defense against his demons, sort of like whistling in the dark. Greene's sense of alienation, his fears, and his obsession with his lost childhood continue to comprise the central themes of his fiction for the rest of his life. Nevertheless, the compulsive act of writing served him well in his lifelong battle with what he calls "the panic fear which is inherent in the human condition." Throughout most of his life he dutifully wrote a minimum of 500 words a day. His manuscripts are filled with notations of word counts: the compulsive act of writing provided him with a sense of psychological equilibrium, but he always had to be on guard for the next onslaught of the demons of his youth and to defend against them with another story, another novel, another trip to a dangerous country to distract him from his plight. He developed an addiction to writing: it became his drug of choice in escaping from the sense of reality he acquired under the sinister influence of Lionel Carter, an unremarkable boy except for his role in unwittingly helping to shape the mind and soul of a distinguished writer.

Twenty-One Stories

"The End of the Party" (probably 1929) is a melodramatic tale that captures the torment and panic experienced by a child due to his secret fear of death. Francis Morton, a highly sensitive child filled with secret fears, tells his protective twin brother, Peter, that he dreamed he died. Listening to his brother relate his frightening dream, Peter has the sense of the whole room darkening and a great bird swooping down upon Francis. The two boys are to attend a party where they will have to play hide-and-seek and Francis, because he is afraid of the dark and senses that something bad will happen to him at the party, clings to the naive hope that God will somehow intercede to save him from having to go. His nurse and his mother, however, eventually prevail and Francis is forced to go to the party. When the children announce that they will play hide-and-seek, Peter sees "a great bird darken his brother's face with its wings."[15] In order to comfort his brother, who is hiding in a corner during the game, Peter takes his hand. Francis is so startled by his brother's touch that he dies of fright. Too young to understand the paradox, Peter "wondered with an obscure self-pity why it was that the pulse of his brother's fear went on and on, when Francis was now where he had always been told there was no more terror and no more darkness" (*CS*, 562).

This story arises out of Greene's own uncomfortable childhood. He was always afraid of the dark, of birds, bats, and strange footsteps. Furthermore, as a young boy he felt isolated from the adult world and began to lead a covert life, keeping certain facts from his parents. He kept secret from his mother, for example, the fact that he had learned to read so that she would not send him off to preparatory school. Francis Morton, the character with whom Greene clearly identifies himself, can only confide in his twin brother. He sees the adult world, represented by his mother and his nurse, as incapable of understanding his fears and therefore "he couldn't bring himself to lay bare his last secrets and end reserve between his mother and himself" (*CS*, 556). Despite his age, Francis is sensitive to the duplicity of adults: "he knew how they taught . . . that there was nothing to fear in death, and how fearfully they avoided the idea of it" (*CS*, 555).

As a child, Greene apparently could not confide in his own brothers and felt, like Francis, terribly isolated by nightmarish fears. Peter Morton is thus a kind of projection of Greene's fantasy of the ideal brother. In the story he functions as a superior clone of Francis: "To address Peter was to speak to his [Francis's] own image in a mirror, an image a little altered by a flaw in the glass, so as to throw back less a likeness of what he was than of what he wishes to be, what he would be without his unreasoning fear of darkness, footsteps of strangers, the flight of bats in dusk-filled gardens" (*CS*, 556).

In a real sense, Francis has been fatally betrayed by the ignorance of adults, who falsely assured him that there was nothing to fear in the dark. The story ends, in fact, with Peter trying to understand why his brother's pulse continues to race when he is "now where he had always been told there was no more terror and no more darkness" (*CS*, 562). In another sense, however, Francis is the victim of a self-fulfilling prophesy. He has convinced himself that something dreadful will happen to him in the dark and having nurtured his terror throughout the day of the party, he makes himself extraordinarily susceptible to his final panic. The irony in his death having been brought about by his brother's supportive touch enriches the opening of the story, where Peter wakes Francis from the dream in which he dies.

In "The Second Death" (1929) Greene approaches the subject of death from a religious angle by introducing the Lazarus theme. This is the first time this theme appears in his work, although he was to use it again in the novel *The End of the Affair* (1952) and the play *The Potting Shed* (1957). Having converted to Catholicism in 1926, Greene was beginning to exploit for his fiction the more dramatic doctrines of his new faith; here he makes imaginative use of the belief in miracles and the resurrection of the body.

The unnamed narrator of this story is called to the deathbed of his friend, a man in his 30s who has lived under the domination of his widowed mother. He explains to the narrator that years earlier, when he was a boy, he became ill and was pronounced dead. It was only when he was being carried out to be buried that the doctor noticed he was alive. While he was dead, he explains, he saw people around him who knew everything he had done wrong—the money he had stolen from his mother, the many girls he had slept with—and so death, he feels, is not a restful peace but a nightmare of guilt. He begs his friend to reassure him that his first death was merely a bad dream, that miracles like that do not happen nowadays, because "You don't know what things were going to happen to me in that dream. And they'd be worse now. . . . When one's dead there's no unconsciousness any more for ever" (*CS*, 549–50).

The last words of the dying man concern stories he has heard of people diseased, crippled, and blind who were restored to health. He desperately wants to be convinced that these are old wives' tales or lies, but before the narrator can answer the man dies. The narrator concludes, "It was a long time ago since I'd thought of that day, ages and ages ago, when I felt a cold touch like spittle on my lids and opening my eyes had seen a man like a tree surrounded by other trees walking away" (*CS*, 550).

In delineating the fears of the dying man, which finally affect his friend, Greene gives an oddball twist to the Lazarus theme. The notion that prevails in this story is that death initiates an eternal nightmare, a disturbing consciousness of failure that will never cease. The dying man's resurrection as a boy serves only to intensify his fear of a second death. The last words of the narrator, quoted above, ambiguously suggest that he too has died (or perhaps been blinded) and subsequently has been miraculously restored. The phrase "a man like a tree surrounded by other trees walking away" conjures up the image of a primitive, Christ-like figure who, having just returned sight to the dead eyes of the narrator, walks with his followers away from another miracle.

Greene describes "I Spy" (1930) as having "simplicity of language, the sense of life as it is lived" (*CS*, viii). Not having to carry the burden of allegory, fantasy, and the supernatural that weighed down his previous stories, "I Spy" is an early landmark in Greene's mastery of the short story form. In this tale he subtly and compellingly refines his obsessive theme of lost innocence.

"I Spy" is the story of a 12-year-old boy, Charlie Stowe (whose name suggests a stowaway), who sneaks downstairs into his father's tobacco shop late at night to smoke a cigarette. In hiding, he sees his father, accompanied by two strangers, enter the shop. Apparently he is being arrested (for spying?), but neither the reader nor Charlie knows exactly what is happening and why.

The masterful quality of this story lies in Greene's description of the boy's instinctive response to the mystery that adult life now presents him: "He remembered how his father had held tight to his collar and fortified himself with proverbs, and he thought for the first time that, while his mother was boisterous and kindly, his father was very like himself, doing things in the dark which frightened him" (*CS*, 537). He now shares with his father a guilty secret half-understood in the darkness and is overwhelmed and isolated by a flood of undefined emotions: fear, betrayal, guilt, and love.

By the skillful use of the third-person narrator, Greene reveals just enough information to allow the reader to participate in the boy's limited perspective, while at the same time providing the reader with insights into the peculiar confusion of the boy's innocent mind tormented by the conflicting emotions of fear and love. In the darkness of the tobacco shop, ironically, the boy begins to see things more clearly. Previously, we are told, Charlie did not love his father: "his father was unreal to him, a wraith, pale, thin, indefinite, who noticed him only spasmodically and left even punishment to his mother" (*CS*, 534). Now the boy recognizes his own childish guilt reflected in the devastating adult reality of his father's arrest, and wishes he could have told him that he loved him. If, as the title of the story hints, the boy's father is being arrested for spying (though Greene does not provide enough details to allow the reader to know the nature of his crime), then the boy's identification with his father while spying in his shop is made even more poignant.

In 1930 Greene submitted a story entitled "Proof Positive" to the *Manchester Guardian* for a ghost-story competition and won the first prize of 10 guineas. Like "The Second Death," this tale plays with the idea of the immortality of the human spirit but does so by ironically emphasizing the horrors of the decaying human body.

A retired army officer, Major Philip Weaver, addressing the local Psychical Society, purports that he will offer positive proof of the immortality of the soul. The old man's speech, however, is incoherent, and he explains to his exasperated audience that he is sick, that he has cancer. The sweet smell of his heavily perfumed handkerchief makes the members uncomfortable. After his speech further degenerates into a series of incomprehensible sounds, he sits down and his head falls backward. A doctor rushes up to him and pronounces him dead, but the doctor is disquieted by the man's appearance: "The body might have been one fished from the sea a long while after death; the flesh of the face seemed as ready to fall as an over-ripe fruit" (*CS*, 542). The doctor then makes a startling announcement: "The man must have been dead a week" (*CS*, 542).

Up to this point the story sounds like a script for "Alfred Hitchcock Presents" or "The Twilight Zone." A man, who turns out to have been dead for a week, speaks to a group of people in order to prove that the spirit is immortal. His proof comes not through his speech but rather through his decayed presence. But Greene adds an interesting cynical note to the tale by means of the character Colonel Crashaw, a hard-headed man of the world: "What the Colonel thought of most was Weaver's claim—'Proof positive'—proof, he had probably meant, that the spirit outlived the body, that it tasted eternity. But all he had certainly revealed was how, without the body's aid, the spirit in seven days decayed into whispered nonsense" (*CS*, 542–43).

Neither "The Second Death" nor the "Proof Positive," then, presents the glorious image of life after death taught by the Catholic church. The powerful emotions of guilt and fear, in the former tale, and the horrific image of the decaying body in the latter, convey Greene's view of life after death as a grotesque nightmare. He reverts to this theme later, in "A Little Place off the Edgeware Road," where the idea of eternity is equated with the rotting flesh of all humanity. Death, in other words, leads to death-in-life, the fearful prospect of the pagan Tithonus rather than the glorious body of the risen Christ.

When Greene joined the Communist party of Great Britain in 1925, he was motivated, according to a friend at the time, by his concern over individual victimization of people rather than by class or wage exploitation (Sherry 1989–, 1:161). Such a view is in keeping with Greene's view of himself as a victim while at Berkhamsted School. Growing somewhat bored with the routines as a student at Oxford, Greene visited the Communist headquarters in Paris in 1926. Although nothing of any political significance resulted from his brief visit, years later he drew upon his flirtatious experience with communism to write the story "Brother."

This story is marred by its eagerness to make the point that the French police, not the Communists, are the true terrorists. The characters are too sketchily drawn, however, to win the reader's interest or sympathy. The chief interest in this story is its disclosure of Greene's early antagonism toward established governments. Throughout his career he portrays the ruling powers as the embodiments of evil and those who oppose those powers as the secular saints. *It's a Battlefield, The Confidential Agent, The Power and the Glory, The Ministry of Fear, The Quiet American, Our Man in Havana, The Comedians,* and *The Human Factor* all assert the idea that established governments, both democracies and dictatorships, are manipulative, cruel, and inhuman, that they will gleefully sacrifice innocent victims in order to maintain their hold on power.

Under the influence of his chief literary mentor, Joseph Conrad, Greene employs the doppelgänger motif for his story "A Day Saved" (1934). The narrator, a schizophrenic named Robinson, becomes so obsessed with a stranger that he pursues him to another country. Although he has followed him like a shadow for days, he fails to understand the motivation behind his own compulsive behavior: "This is the horror I cannot escape: knowing nothing, his name, what it was he carried, why I wanted it so, why I followed him" (*CS*, 528). When the stranger decides to leave the country by plane rather than by train in order to save a day, the narrator becomes furious because he counted on developing a relationship with him during the long train ride. In fact, he even planned his murder "if in no other way he would yield what I wanted" (*CS*, 530).

This story bears an interesting relationship to "The End of the Party" in that both tales focus upon the disparity between twins. Francis Morton envies the fact that his brother, although an identical twin, is not haunted by terrible fears: Peter was "what he wished to be" (*CS*, 556). Like Francis, Robinson is an incomplete personality. He lacks the comfortableness of the stranger's good nature, happiness, and protective stupidity. While they share drinks Robinson acknowledges that he "felt more warmly toward him than toward any other man I have known, for, like love between a man and a woman, my affection was partly curiosity" (*CS*, 531).

Unlike Conrad's protagonists, who achieve a symbolic integration with their doubles in "The Secret Sharer" and *The Heart of Darkness*, Robinson, who is willing to murder to get at the essence of the stranger, remains an incomplete, bitter man, who wishes his double future suffering. It may well be that Greene himself did not at this time have the wherewithal to resolve his own manic-depression states of mind, a failure documented in his narrator's confused account of his obsessive pursuit of an elusive doppelgänger. In later stories, such as "Under the Garden," Greene continues the pursuit of his phantom identity.

On 6 May, 1935 England celebrated the Silver Jubilee of King George V's accession to the throne. Greene took advantage of the occasion by using the event for the setting of his story "Jubilee" (1935). His tale, however, is not about the Jubilee but about a retired madam (who brags that she cleaned up the London streets by opening a house of prostitution) and a 50-year-old gigolo named Chalfont eager to keep up an appearance of gallantry.

Chalfont is typical of Greene's seedy characters. Broke and living in a cheap furnished room, he holes up in his flat during the Jubilee lest he run into some of his former women friends who have come up from the country for the celebration. After the Jubilee Chalfont, dressed in his soiled, shabby-genteel clothes, goes out among the public to practice his "old game" of picking up rich women. Times have changed, however, as the Jubilee itself reminds us, and his accustomed world has mostly vanished. He goes to his usual café where he meets a woman whom he assumes to be rich and engages her in conversation. Ironically, she turns out to be a madam who, having amassed a small fortune, has retired from her profession. Breaking through his pretensions of gentility, she turns the tables on Chalfont and patronizes him through her offer of five pounds to help him over hard times. She also offers him, if he chooses, the opportunity to return to her room so that he can "do [his] stuff" (*CS*, 527). The story ends with her slapping him on the back, saying "Let's have a little Jubilee spirit, dear," as she takes "her revenge for a world of uncongenial partners on old Mr. Chalfont" (*CS*, 527).

The character of the retired madam that Greene introduces in this story is the prototype of several of his later characters, the most notable being Ida Arnold in *Brighton Rock*. Raucous, merry, self-confident, sexually uninhibited, she embodies Greene's conception of the woman with a strong moral code (she cleans up the London streets of prostitutes so that visitors will not get an improper impression of the city) who enjoys a healthy sensuality. Like the self-righteous Ida Arnold, who brings about the destruction of the demonic Pinkie, the madam devastates the phony gallantry and class consciousness of the exploitative Chalfont. As the narrator observes, "You couldn't call him anything else now but old Mr. Chalfont" (*CS*, 527).

In 1936 the *News Chronicle* commissioned Greene to write a story to appear as a five-day serial. Greene thus produced a longer-than-usual short story, "The Basement Room," considered by critics to be one of his best. Drawing upon the painful memories of his own disillusionment as a child, Greene explores the theme of the loss of innocence and the lasting effect on a child's life of a single traumatic event.

This is one of the earliest stories to dramatize Greene's recurrent theme of crossing borders, of moving from a safe world to one fraught with danger. In his parents' absence Philip Lane has been left in the care of the butler and his wife, Mr. and Mrs. Baines. Seven-year-old Philip for the first time in his life enters the basement where the servants live. He "vibrated with the strange, the new experience." "This is life" (*CS*, 458), he thinks, but as the story proves, life turns out to be death, both for Mrs. Baines and for his own innocence.

Philip admires Baines because he "had seen the world." He fills the boy's head with stories of his adventures in far-off and exotic places. Mrs. Baines, in contrast, resembles the witch in the nursery of whom Greene once dreamed. She is a domineering figure who nags her husband and threatens Philip. The boy, of course, does not understand the relationship between these adults, but he gets a painful insight into it one day when he discovers Baines in a restaurant with a strange girl. "He would never escape that scene" because he never understood it. "It conditioned his career, the long austerity of his life; when he was dying, rich and alone, it was said that he asked: 'Who is she?'" (*CS*, 465). Baines tells him that she is his niece, but the reader knows her to be his mistress.

"Caught up in other people's darkness" (*CS*, 467), Philip is now thrust into the adult world of secrets and lies as he becomes a pawn in the match between Mr. and Mrs. Baines. Philip "would have nothing to do with their secrets, the responsibilities they were determined to lay upon him" (*CS*, 470). But one day Baines has the girl, Emmy, visit him when Mrs. Baines is away, and his infidelity is discovered when she returns unexpectedly. Philip is suddenly caught up in the powerful tension in the house and he protests: "It wasn't fair, the walls were down again between his world and theirs . . . ; a passion moved in the house he recognized but could not understand" (*CS*, 477–78). And thus, "Life fell on him with savagery" (*CS*, 478). Baines struggles with his wife, who, like a cartoon of an evil witch, falls over the banister in a flurry of black clothes to her death. The world of the nursery dies also: "the whole house has been turned over to the grown-up world" (*CS*, 479).

When the police arrive, Philip, exhausted by trying to untangle the web of secrets and lies thrown upon him, tells what he has seen and cries out that "It was all Emmy's fault." The constable asks Baines, "who is she?"—the same question that is to haunt Philip even to his deathbed. The simple, trusting, hero-worshipping mind of the child has been shattered in the dark underworld of the basement room. Philip could live happily with the bifurcation of good and evil as embodied in Mr. and Mrs. Baines, respectively, but the powerful ambiguity presented in Emmy and her relationship to Baines burned deeply into Philip's mind and changes the course of his life.

Philip's passage through the green baize door that leads to the basement room where Baines and his wife live is richly symbolic. The contrasting worlds of upstairs and downstairs convey a social hierarchy familiar to the English. Secluded from the servants' mysterious lives by the conventions of his class, Philip naturally finds the opportunity to escape from his dull routines and to enter their world an exhilarating prospect. The two levels also suggest the conscious and unconscious realms, a duality that Greene reverts to in "Under the Garden." The other side of the green baize door leads to a dangerous, alien underworld, akin to the subconscious with its potential for evil. The disparate areas of the nursery and the basement also symbolize innocence and experience; Philip's descent into the latter marks his irrevocable loss of simple childhood joy.

Besides the mythic theme of the fall into experience and the Jungian archetypes of heaven and hell, Greene works the powerful theme of betrayal into the fabric of his story. Under the enormous and unreasoning pressure to keep adult secrets, Philip finally betrays Baines, whom he loves, to the police: "He wasn't going to keep any more secrets: he was going to finish once and for all with everything, with Baines and Mrs. Baines and the grown-up life beyond him" (*CS*, 488). This passage recalls Greene's own torment when he was a student at Berkhamsted and had to choose between loyalty to his headmaster father or to his fellow students. The guilt and pain of betrayal were never forgotten and, like Coleridge's Ancient Mariner, Greene recreates his experience over and over again in his stories and novels.

In 1935 Greene, in search of adventure, made the first of his several exploratory trips to distant and dangerous places. He and his 23-year-old cousin, Barbara Greene, went to Liberia, an area of Africa little known to most Europeans, who saw it as a place of cannibalism and witchcraft. During the arduous journey through the jungle, Greene became seriously ill with fever and almost died. Greene recorded his adventures in a diary, later published as *Journey without Maps* (1936). He also worked some of his experiences, including his near-fatal illness and his confrontation with his native carriers, into a short story entitled "A Chance for Mr. Lever," published in the *London Mercury*.

"A Chance for Mr. Lever" represents the adult dream of peace, freedom, and home in a world hostile to fantasy. For 30 years Mr. Lever sold heavy machinery in Europe and the United States, but now he finds himself in Africa with his home in Eastbourne only a pleasant memory. His mission is to find a man who will enable him to make a great deal of money by authorizing a contract for earth-moving equipment. Enduring the squalor and heat of the journey, he finally discovers his man, but too late, for his client has just died from yellow fever. "It seemed at first to be the end of everything, of his journey, his hopes, his life with Emily" (*CS*, 505).

It is the image of his wife Emily that continues to sustain him through his ordeal. Like so many of Greene's heroes, Mr. Lever requires one personal relationship to give meaning and shape to his life, and now even that is threatened by its remoteness. It is interesting to note that Greene decided to travel in Liberia in order to escape not only his growing sense of boredom but his responsibility of caring for his one-year-old daughter, all too happily left behind with his wife in England. Quite possibly Mr. Lever's concern for Emily reflects Greene's guilt for leaving his wife at such a critical time, a guilt magnified during his fever when he thought he might die.

Suddenly all of Mr. Lever's conventional views are undermined by his awareness of mortality. Pondering the solemnity of death, he asserts that "death wasn't solemn: it was a lemon-yellow skin and a black vomit" (*CS*, 507). All of the moral clichés of his past, such as "Honesty is the best policy," lose their meaning. Only his devotion to his wife moves him forward now: he and she *must* survive, so he forges a letter from the dead man ordering a shipment of the heavy machinery. Mr. Lever has apparently won his battle. He will be wealthy now and can return home to Eastbourne to live happily with Emily. He is free at last from the restraints that held him through a long and unrewarding career. The reader discovers in the last paragraph, however, that the mosquito that bit the dead man has also bitten Mr. Lever and that along with the forged order he carries back with him through the jungle he also carries a fatal dose of yellow fever. A kindly god, if there is a god, the narrator says, "was ready to give Mr. Lever three days of happiness, three days off the galling chain" (*CS*, 509) before he died.

Thus the African jungle becomes an ironic place of innocence for the hero. He has found the mystical peace and joy of childhood, but his paradise is imaginary, a mirage that the reader knows will soon vanish as a result of a mere mosquito bite. Happiness, like innocence, is at best a dream for the adult, and one's attempt to capture it results in anguish or self-deception. Greene develops the theme of this story much more fully in his two African novels, *The Heart of the Matter* and

A Burnt-Out Case, setting his protagonists, Scobie and Querry, on the same hopeless, adult quest for the simple peace and joy of childhood. The African setting, suggestive of an exotic garden of Eden, reveals itself to be a fool's paradise, a simple, primitive land that gives way to corruption, evil, and mortality.

Having himself attempted to commit suicide on several occasions, Greene had a natural and compelling interest in the subject of self-destruction. Several of his works, such as *Brighton Rock* (1938), *The Heart of the Matter* (1948), and *The Potting Shed* (1957) focus upon suicidal characters. His short story "A Drive in the Country" (1937) is his first notable attempt to embody this dramatic and personal subject in fiction. A flawed story, it nevertheless allowed Greene to distance himself from, and thereby put into perspective, his depressive self. More important, the story contained the germ for his brilliant novel, *Brighton Rock*, which he published the following year.

A young girl, fed up with the meticulous regularity and materialism of her father, plans to run away with her boyfriend, Fred. "She wanted to match the old reckless quality of Fred's mind" (*CS*, 435) and, like Pinkie's girlfriend, Rose, in *Brighton Rock*, she surrenders her will to the strange and exhilarating events that lie ahead of her. She and Fred drive off to the country where he surprises her by proposing a suicide pact. "Life's hell. There's nothing we can do" (*CS*, 442) he argues, and like Pinkie, "he was like a skilled logician; he knew all the stages of the argument" (*CS*, 443).

Despite his protestations of love, he cannot convince the girl to commit suicide: she lacks the mad compassion and trust of Rose and backs off. Fred, nevertheless, goes into the woods and shoots himself. The initial excitement of escaping from her parents and running off with a dangerous young man vanishes, and she is suddenly terrified. She flees home with the awareness that she "had wanted a little of both worlds: irresponsibility and a safe love, danger and a secure heart" (*CS*, 445). The story ends with the assurance that "she could feel nothing but gladness that she had escaped from him" (*CS*, 447) and that "She was quite free from pain" (*CS*, 450).

This story is interesting as a preliminary sketch of Pinkie and Rose. Fred's character is vague and his reckless desire to destroy himself and the girl poorly motivated. The girl's refusal to trust Fred merely underscores the shallowness of their relationship. She is fascinated with the idea of rebelliousness but is not herself a true rebel. By the time he wrote *Brighton Rock* Greene had discovered the key to his narrative and thematic problems. He makes Rose totally committed to Pinkie and allots the need for safety and security to another character, Ida Arnold, a woman who enjoys a good time but never experiences the anguish of true love.

When he was a student at Berkhamsted School Greene and several of the other boys became infatuated with the beautiful daughter of one of the schoolmasters. Later, while at Oxford, Greene's affections turned toward a young girl named Rose, a waitress at a local restaurant. Norman Sherry (1989–, 1:178) speculates that Greene's feelings for these two girls may have provided the inspiration for his story "The Innocent" (1937).

The narrator, accompanied by Lola, a girl he picked up in a bar, returns to his childhood home in the country. Lola, with her cheap perfume and city ways, stands in contrast to "the smell of innocence" (*CS*, 452) in the village and to the young girl the narrator was in love with as a child. He goes to a hole in a gate where he once left secret messages for his childhood sweetheart and discovers one of his old messages still there. He examines it and is shocked to find "a picture of crude obscenity" (*CS*, 456), a childishly inaccurate sketch of a man and a woman in a sexual posture. Feeling at first betrayed and wondering if Lola is really so much out of place here after all, the narrator later realizes that the drawing has a "deep innocence": "I had believed I was drawing something with a meaning and beautiful; it is only now after thirty years of life that the picture seemed obscene" (*CS*, 456).

The story, derived from Greene's revisitation of Berkhamsted, the place of his birth, develops the contrast between the innocence of youthful eroticism and the corruption of adult lust through a first-person narrator. Reminiscent of Wordsworth's "Tintern Abbey," in which the poet takes the measure of his maturity by revisiting the simple countryside familiar to his youth, "The Innocent" underscores the mystery of lost innocence that cannot be fully penetrated by the adult mind. The child may be father of the man, as Wordsworth says, but Greene's story suggests that child and man, like Dr. Jekyll and Mr. Hyde, while residing in one body, are irrevocably disparate personalities.

Ever since he first read D. H. Lawrence's *The Plumed Serpent*, when he was 21 years old, Greene had dreamed of visiting Mexico. He finally got his chance in 1938. His extensive travels throughout the country during a time of religious persecution rejuvenated Greene's creative energy: his Mexican experiences were the wellspring for three works: a travel book, *The Lawless Roads* (1939), a novel, *The Power and the Glory* (1940), and a short story, "Across the Bridge" (1938).

In writing "Across the Bridge" Greene developed one of his recurrent symbols: the border, the thin geographical and psychological line between sanctuary and danger, boredom and excitement, and life and death.

Greene experiments with his point of view in this tale by making his narrator a self-conscious storyteller. The unnamed narrator, a newcomer to the Mexican border town and unable to speak the language, attempts to put together the story of another recent arrival, Mr. Calloway, an English businessman reportedly worth a million dollars. Calloway apparently gained his wealth through his dishonest investments and has come to Mexico where he enjoys temporary sanctuary from extradition proceedings. Unable to spend his money, knowing no Spanish, and with a dog as his only companion, Calloway is a lonely, frustrated, and alien figure about whom the narrator and other villagers speculate at great length. With his limited and tentative knowledge of the facts, the narrator transforms Calloway's past and his comings and goings into a story. Throughout his account are such remarks as "I don't know how to treat this story" (*CS*, 422) and "That earlier part of the story was, I suppose, dramatic, but I didn't watch it and I can't invent what I haven't seen" (*CS*, 422).

Greene admired the ease with which Dickens used the first-person narrator in *Great Expectations*, but recognized its limitations and difficulties and only became comfortable with it during the 1950s and 1960s, where he used it for such novels as *The End of the Affair* (1951), *The Quiet American* (1955), and *The Comedians* (1966). The narrators of those three novels are not entirely reliable. The narrator of "Across the Bridge," however, is a transitional figure in Greene's developing narrative technique. He openly acknowledges his ignorance of his subject but proposes to do his honest best in providing an outsider's point of view on the actions that unfold before him. The main thrust of his narrative is to disclose a "human being's capacity for self-deception, our baseless optimism that is so much more appalling than our despair" (*CS*, 432).

"The Case for the Defence" (1939) is notable chiefly for its cleverness and its surprise ending. The narrator is an experienced court reporter who arouses our interest with his opening sentence: "It was the strangest murder trial I ever attended" (*CS*, 407). A man named

Adams, accused of murder, faces several eyewitnesses who testify they saw him leaving the scene of the crime. "It was all over, you would have said, but the hanging" (*CS*, 408), the narrator observes. Counsel for the defense, however, remarkably pleads a case of mistaken identity. He asks Mrs. Salmon, the Crown's chief witness, to identify the man she claims to have seen the night of the murder. In the back of the court Adams's twin brother stands up and the witness can no longer swear that it was the man in the dock whom she saw. And so, Adams is acquitted for lack of evidence.

Greene then adds a final twist to his story: one of the twins, upon leaving the courthouse, is run down by an automobile. Moreover, his skull is crushed just as the murder victim's had been. The narrator speculates: "Divine vengeance? I wish I knew" (*CS*, 411). The other Mr. Adams, rising from next to the body of his dead brother, glares at Mrs. Salmon: "He was crying, but whether he was the murderer or the innocent man nobody will ever be able to tell. But if you were Mrs. Salmon, could you sleep at night?" (*CS*, 411).

Greene's use of the first-person narrator here is less accomplished than in "Across the Bridge." While Greene allows the narrator of the latter story to lapse into omniscience, he nevertheless provides him with a cynical outlook on life that gives shape to his account of a man ironically trapped by his ambitions. The reporter in "A Case for the Defence," however, adds little to the story that a third-person narrator could not have achieved. The passage quoted above, which concludes the story, emphasizes the obvious. We hardly need to be told that the surviving twin presents an ambiguous terror to Mrs. Salmon, and we certainly do not need to be asked the melodramatic final question.

Greene clearly was fascinated by twins, a theme I noted earlier with regard to "The End of the Party" and "A Day Saved." These tales clearly owe something to the more sophisticated psychological studies of doubles in the works of Robert Louis Stevenson and Joseph Conrad. More interesting, however, is the question as to why Greene was so interested in the doppelgänger motif in these two authors. The answer lies in Greene's own psychology: his recognition of his manic-depressive personality and his cultivation of that personality in his writings. Furthermore, Greene's childhood sense of betrayal finds an analogue in the works of Stevenson and Conrad.

Greene's puritanical revulsion at the human body underlies the theme of "A Little Place off the Edgeware Road" (1939). The hero of this story is a man named Craven, a name that both suggests his cowardice and recalls the character of Raven, the sexually repressed hired killer in *A Gun for Sale*. All the way to the park Craven "was reminded of passion but you needed money for love. All that a poor man could get was lust" (*CS*, 412). Craven carries his body "like something he hated" and recalls a recurrent dream: "he has been alone in the huge cavernous burying ground of all the world. Every grave was connected to another under the ground: the globe was honeycombed for the sake of the dead, and on each occasion of dreaming he had discovered anew the horrifying fact that the body doesn't decay" (*CS*, 412–13).

Intrigued by dreams, Greene here portrays the ultimate Swiftian nightmare, the immortalization of the human body with all of its disgusting defects. Craven is repulsed at the thought that "There are no worms and dissolution. Under the ground the world was littered with masses of dead flesh ready to rise again with their warts and boils and eruptions" (*CS*, 413).

When Craven enters a motion picture theater, a small bearded man sits next to him and begins to speak what sounds like nonsense. Piecing events together, Craven decides that the man must be the murderer in a recent tragedy of which he had read. He calls the police to report the man: they inform him that they already have the murderer in custody but that the body of the victim has disappeared.

Recalling the sticky hand that the man in the theater had laid on his leg, Craven is "back in the horror of his dream—the squalid darkening street was only one of the innumerable tunnels connecting grave to grave where the imperishable bodies lay" (*CS*, 419). He tries to convince himself that he is dreaming, but when he looks into a mirror he sees tiny drops of blood on his face, and he screams out, "I won't go mad. I'm sane. I won't go mad" (*CS*, 419). But a crowd gathers around him, and soon a policeman arrives, apparently to carry him off to an insane asylum.

The conclusion weakens this story because it should already be clear to the reader that Craven's view of the world is a mad and obsessive one, that he is locked into a nightmare that torments his waking life. It would have been better if Greene had ended the tale with the idea that Craven was "back in the horror of his dream." One does not really care if he is sane or not, but his nightmare about the dead and living is of considerable interest. As Greene himself noted, "Sometimes identification with a character goes so far that one may dream his dream, and not one's own" (*CS*, xii).

In light of the repulsion toward the human body repeatedly exhibited by characters in his novels and stories, one suspects Greene may well have dreamed the dream of Craven. In *A Gun for Sale* (1936) and *Brighton Rock* (1938), the heroes Raven and Pinkie express their fear of sexuality through violence. Furthermore, Raven's features are marred by an ugly harelip, a disfigurement that helps drive his hatred and distrust of women. The focus upon the stench of Major Weaver's decaying body, veiled by perfume, in "Proof Positive" is still another instance of Greene's puritanical castigation of the mortal flesh. His brahmin sense of cleanliness may in part be an explanation for his attitude. As he explains in his autobiography, when he was at Berkhamsted School he felt that he was imprisoned in an excremental enclosure in which he had to endure "the struggle of conflicting loyalties, the sense of continuous grime, of unlocked lavatory doors, the odor of farts (it was sexually a very pure house, there was no hint of homosexuality, but scatology was another matter, and I have disliked the lavatory joke from that age on)" (*Sort*, 71).

Greene's sense of humor frequently turned upon bodily functions. In *Our Man in Havana* (1958), for example, there is a hilarious scene in which Hawthorne, a British agent, takes Jim Wormold into a lavatory where he attempts to recruit him as a spy. The eccentric physician in "Doctor Crombie" (1965) lectures children that masturbation causes cancer. "Alas, Poor Maling" (1940) is one of the earliest examples of Greene distancing himself from the grotesque oddities of the human body by employing humor.

A printer named Maling is cursed with a peculiar form of indigestion that causes his stomach to replicate sounds that it "hears." When he is at a party, for example, his stomach picks up the music from an adjacent dance orchestra and, to his embarrassment, quietly replays it during a moment of silence. At a later date, during the height of the war with Germany, he attends an important meeting at which his employer and representatives of another newsprint company are arranging a merger. Just as they are about to sign the papers, Maling's stomach reproduces the sound of an air-raid siren (they had been going off during the previous days) and the executives rush for the shelter, where they remain for 12 hours. Rather than trying to explain, Maling says nothing. The next day he drops out of sight, never to be heard from again. As the narrator observes, Maling's stomach effectively picked up the air-raid warning, but "it had somehow never taken to the All Clear" (*CS*, 406).

"Men at Work" (1941) is also set in London during the war and reflects Greene's sense of boredom and uselessness while working at the Ministry of Information. Told from the omniscient point of view, the story details the empty routines of Richard Skate and other members of the Book Committee of the Ministry of Information. Skate, who had originally aspired to be a playwright, has happily adjusted to his life as as civil servant. At the conclusion of another paper-shuffling committee meeting, Skate opens one of the building's large windows and looks out to see heroic RAF pilots returning to their bases after a sortie: "Far up in the pale enormous sky little white lines, like the phosphorescent spoor of snails, showed where men were going home after work" (*CS*, 401).

Greene, with his ambition to be a novelist, projects his failed, depressed self in the person of Skate. After postponing his dreams and seeing his creativity threatened by the dull security of life as a civil servant, Greene realized he had to strike out for a new territory lest he become another Skate. He joined the Secret Service and went off to West Africa. Skate, in contrast, must settle for his final vision of British pilots returning home after engagements with German fighter planes. The world of actual combat appears unrelated to the rhetoric and self-sustaining bureaucracy of the Ministry of Information. Skate's sighting of the returning pilots underscores the irony of the story's title by making a distinction between make-work and real work.

A third story set during the war, "When Greek Meets Greek" (1941), is a lighthearted comedy about fraud. Exploiting the fact that the war effort has made it impossible for many young people to attend university, Mr. Fennick and his niece, Elizabeth, set up a phony school called St. Ambrose's College, Oxford, that offers examinations and degrees by correspondence. An ex-con named Driver, whose name is identical to a noted Lord Driver, enrolls his son, Frederick, recently released from prison, in St. Ambrose's. Having no money, Driver arranges for his son's education on the credit of his aristocratic name. After the graduation ceremony, which Fennick conducts in a London hotel, Elizabeth suspects that Driver, like her uncle, is a swindler. She and Frederick, after going off together and confessing their mutual fraud, decide to get married and to outdo the old frauds by taking over the college business.

Despite the frivolous tone of his story, Greene manages to weave into it a serious criticism of the British government, especially the Ministry of Information. Elizabeth justifies her involvement in her uncle's crooked scheme by thinking "They were not reducing supplies like the Ministry of Food, or destroying confidence like the Ministry of Information" (*CS*, 383). Later, when she and Fred decide to outwit their mentors, Greene notes that "There were bigger frauds all round them: officials of the Ministries passed carrying little portfolios; controllers of this and that purred by in motor-cars, and men with the big blank faces of advertisement hoardings strode purposefully in khaki with scarlet tabs down Park Lane from the Dorchester" (*CS*, 392).

By the end of the 1940s Greene had written several novels dealing with Catholicism, but "The Hint of an Explanation" (1949) is the first short story in which he focuses upon Catholic subject matter. It is an ironic story about a young Catholic boy whose faith is strengthened by the town atheist. Like "The Basement Room," this story makes the point that a single event in a child's life can dramatically affect his future.

Greene employs a first-person narrator in order to arrange a surprise ending for the story. On a long train journey the narrator listens to the account of his fellow traveler, a man named David, about an incident in his childhood that give him a hint of an explanation about God's mysterious ways. The narrator, who resembles Greene during his agnostic Oxford days, says that "I have a certain intuition (which I do not trust, founded as it may well be on childish experiences and needs) that God exists, and I am surprised occasionally into belief by the extraordinary coincidences that beset our path like the traps set for leopards in the jungle, but intellectually I am revolted at the whole notion of such a God who can so abandon his creatures to the enormities of Free Will" (*CS*, 362). The skeptical narrator is thus the perfect audience for David's ironic story of religious faith, for the story itself is structured like a providential trap.

David's tale has some of the features of a fairy tale: an innocent boy heroically overpowers a threatening monster and is rewarded for his bravery. A terrifying character named Blacker, a baker by trade, bribes David with an electric train set if he will bring him the Communion Host. Obsessed with his atheism, Blacker wants to examine the Host to prove once and for all that Christ's body and blood are not there. Driven by his fear of Blacker and his desire for the train set, the boy goes to Communion and lodges the Host under his tongue. When he is alone, he wraps the Host in a piece of newspaper and carries it home so that he can give it to Blacker the next day.

For the first time the boy begins to realize through Blacker's obsession that the Host, which he previously took for granted each Sunday, was something special indeed: "I knew that this which I had beside my bed was something of infinite value—something a man would pay for with his whole peace of mind, something that was so hated one could love it as one loves an outcast or a bullied child" (*CS*, 373). And so, David swallows the Host at the last minute instead of turning it over to Blacker. "Then something happened," recalls David, "which seemed to me now more terrible than his desire to corrupt or my thoughtless act: he began to weep" (*CS*, 374).

After David finishes his story and as the narrator's account draws to a conclusion, the narrator gets a surprise glimpse of a priest's collar beneath David's overcoat. David's earlier remark about a hint of an explanation suddenly makes sense both to the narrator and to the reader: the demonic Blacker, filled with hatred and finally with the anguish of frustration, has led the indifferent boy into the powerful mysteries of his own religion.

Greene employs this same irony in *The End of the Affair* where the atheist preacher, Smythe, though his relentless hatred of God, unwittingly brings Sarah into the Catholic church. In light of such irony and of the religious roles played by adversaries in Christian providence, Greene's atheistic characters function with a significant ambiguity. From the child's point of view, Blacker is a simple villain, an oppressive force that threatens the sanctity of the Host. As an instrument of God's providence, however, he becomes the catalyst of the boy's faith. He is thus portrayed with a muffled sympathy. The Catholics in the village do not patronize his bakery because he is a freethinker. He is ugly, having only one walleye and a turnip-shaped head, and is unmarried with no family. When, at the end of the story, David swallows the Host, we see Blacker break down and hopelessly weep like a child. It may be that Blacker is possessed by Satan (or the "Thing," as David prefers to call him), which would allow us to see him as pure evil, but his grotesquely flawed body and mind permit us also to pity him, especially in light of his unwitting service to the God he denied.

A chilling account of violence, "The Destructors" (1954) is one of Greene's best-known and most discussed stories. The hero is a boy named Trevor, the son of a former architect now turned clerk, who takes over a local gang of hoodlums through his outrageous plan of demolition. Trevor has acquired his father's keen sense of architectural splendor, but paradoxically his reaction to beauty is destructive.

Having been invited into the house of an old man named Thomas (known as "Old Misery" to the gang), Trevor is fascinated by the antiquity and design of the house, built by the famous architect, Christopher Wren.

Trevor gains the leadership of his gang by means of his exciting plan to destroy Old Misery's house. When the old man leaves town for the weekend, the gang proceeds under Trevor's masterful supervision to remove the plumbing, wires, fixtures, and floors, so that only the walls of the building remain. Trevor achieves the status of a destructive artist directing a virtuoso performance. Old Misery, meanwhile, returns home unexpectedly, and Trevor for the moment "had no words as his dreams shook and slid" (*CS*, 340). But he arranges to lock the old man in the outhouse located in the backyard until he completes his destruction. He ties a rope between a supporting beam of the house and a parked cab. The next morning when the cabby drives off to work, the house comes crashing down. The driver, hearing Old Misery's shouts, releases him from the outhouse, and the old man sobs out, "Where's my house?" The cabby simply laughs at the absurdity of the situation. Greene writes: "One moment the house had stood there with such dignity between the bomb-sites like a man in a top hat, and then, bang, crash, there wasn't anything left—not anything" (*CS*, 346).

Greene successfully works the sense of his own lost childhood into the character of Trevor who, we are told, acts "with the fury of the child he had never been" (*CS*, 339). Like the teenage hoodlum Pinkie in *Brighton Rock*, Trevor is a violent youth who is filled with rage and at the same time possessed of a moral code. When Trevor discovers Old Misery's savings and Blackie, the deposed gangleader, asks him if he is going to share the money, Trevor replies: "We aren't thieves. . . . Nobody's going to steal anything from this home" (*CS*, 337). He then methodically burns the banknotes, one by one.

Whereas Greene describes Pinkie's past with enough detail to make his violent behavior somewhat understandable, he reveals very little about Trevor's motivations. The few details he does provide, however, are of considerable interest. We learn that Trevor's father is "a former architect and present clerk" who "had 'come down in the world' and that his mother considered herself better than the neighbours" (*CS*, 327). Greene makes it clear that Trevor's destruction of the house is not motivated by hatred of Old Misery: "Of course I don't hate him," he says to Blackie. "There'd be no fun if I hated him" (*CS*, 338).

What, then, is the source of fun for Trevor in his bizarre act of destruction? It is evident that Trevor does not understand his own motivation. All he knows is a powerful compulsion to destroy this beautiful, historical house. His use of the word "beautiful" interestingly sets him apart from the other boys. Blackie detects in Trevor's use of the word the threat of the upper class and almost sasses him with "My dear Trevor, old chap" (*CS*, 331). One of Trevor's pleasures comes from the destruction of a symbol of his own class and he manipulates with revolutionary zeal his unimaginative, lower-class fellows. That this elegant house continues to stand amidst the rubble of the blitz is an affront to him. Like the last, unfallen domino, it must be toppled. Despite his darkened innocence, Trevor's character and actions offer a complex symbolic significance to Greene and his readers.

The narrator says that "destruction after all is a form of creation. A kind of imagination had seen this house as it had become" (*CS*, 337). This view suggests dadaism or political nihilism. Trevor's destruction of the house could be seen as a satire of the creative process or as a political and social commentary upon Europe in the 1940s. Old Misery's house is a symbol of civilization. Like St. Paul's Cathedral, also designed by Wren, it is one of the few structures to survive the blitz. By destroying it now, Trevor, in his microcosm of London, brings to a logical conclusion the leveling of European civilization wrought by Hitler's army.

Trevor's obsession with the house and its dismantling, however, cannot be explained simply in terms of esthetics or social satire. On the psychological level, Trevor's attack upon the house suggests his (and Greene's?) hostility toward his father and toward a society that fails to reward someone of his class. Trevor's obsession with the house is enhanced by his knowledge of its eminent designer and by its 200-year-old spiral staircase (an image used in "The Basement Room" to symbolize the link between innocence and experience). The house is an appropriate symbol of Trevor's father, a designer of houses, and may also represent the more heavenly house noted in the Bible: "In my Father's house there are many mansions." Like the demonic Pinkie, Trevor symbolically lashes out at both his biological and heavenly fathers, who have betrayed him into a fallen world. Dadaist, nihilist, fallen angel, and player in the oedipal triangle, Trevor remains a wonderfully ambiguous character.

Underlying the serious themes of this story is an important comic element. When Old Misery returns home unexpectedly, Trevor locks him in his outdoor privy and thoughtfully provides him with penny buns, sausage rolls, and a blanket. The last scene in the story comes close to slapstick as the cabdriver unwittingly brings the frame of the house crashing to the ground. Greene even works a prophetic pun into the story when Old Misery says his horoscope warns him to be wary of any dealings because of a "danger of serious crash" (*CS*, 343). The cabdriver is convulsed with laughter at the sight of the fallen ruins and tells Old Misery, "I'm sorry. I can't help it, Mr. Thomas. There's nothing personal, but you've got to admit it's funny" (*CS*, 346).

The unsettling humor of this story is that of the armchair anarchist, who delights in the comic violence while enjoying the protection and comfortable amenities of middle-class society. It is the same dark eye that sees comedy in the beheading of Father Christmas by a helicopter blade in "Dear Dr. Falkenheim," in Pinkie's sadistic message of hatred left for his trusting wife, Rose, in *Brighton Rock*, and in Querry's ironic murder in *A Burnt-Out Case*. Greene's cynical humor has several facets. It is an expression of despair that grows out of the unjust, bombed-out world of children who learn to parrot and parody the violence of their leaders. It is also the expression of manic and adolescent elation at having attained freedom through the symbolic destruction of civilization (the shaping and controlling father figure). With the destruction of the old order there is the deferred fantasy of building a new, unhampered life out of the rubble.

It is as if Greene re-creates through Trevor his own rage against his father and society. In seeking vengeance for his stolen childhood, he adopts the black-comic mode as a means of distancing himself from the experience. The humor, however, reinforces in the reader the horror of violence and disorder. It is the humor bequeathed to Anthony Burgess who, in *A Clockwork Orange*, resurrects the spirit of Trevor for his comic-brutal hero, Alex.

There may be even another dimension to Greene's submerged psychology in this story. Norman Sherry says that the house in "The Destructors" is based on the house Greene and his wife rented in 1938. Built in 1730, it was located in Clapham Common, and, according to Sherry, "It was to be the last house they lived in together and it was to be destroyed by a bomb during the blitz in London during the Second World War" (1989–, 1:569). While Sherry draws no inferences from his observation, one may see in Trevor's methodical dismantling of the house a comment on Greene's disintegrating marriage to Vivien. Years earlier Greene had proposed, perhaps rashly, a celibate marriage in order to accommodate Vivien's fear of sexuality. As Greene eventually planned to sever his monastic relationship with his wife and live apart, what better way of obliterating that part of his life than the symbolic destruction of the last house in which they lived together? Greene's previous romanticization of Vivien's frigidity appears to have gradually faded and to have been replaced by a growing but repressed hostility.

"The Blue Film" (1954), written about the time of "The Destructors," dealing explicitly with a frigid wife and a sexually unhappy husband, gives added credibility to the marital interpretation of the latter story. Set in Indochina, which Greene visited in 1954, "The Blue Film" is about a man named Carter, who has taken his unhappy wife with him on a business trip. As she complains about her boredom: "If you weren't with *me*," she whines, "you'd find . . . you know what I mean, Spots" (*CS*, 355). Carter, meanwhile, observes her damaged beauty: "she has reached an age when the satisfied woman is at her most beautiful, but the lines of discontent had formed" (*CS*, 355). His next thought is especially revealing about Greene's relationship with Vivien: "It was sad how when one was young, one so often mistook the signs of frigidity for a kind of distinction" (*CS*, 355). In a letter to Vivien before their marriage Greene wrote, "What I long for is a quite original marriage with you. . . . There'd be no domestic tying down, & you'd always keep your ideal of celibacy, & you could help me to keep the same ideal" (quoted in Sherry 1989–, 1:201). Later he wrote her, "I wonder if you'll be really happy with me. Sometimes I think you are too fine for love, I mean human love" (quoted in Sherry, 1989–, 1:342).

Carter agrees to find a spot for their mutual entertainment and hires a guide who brings the couple to a wooden hut where old, amateurish pornographic films are shown. Carter and his wife are mutually embarrassed, but Mrs. Carter, while revolted at what she is seeing, nevertheless insists upon staying. She is amazed to discover her husband in one of the old films. Carter explains that he acted in the picture 30 years ago for the fun and because the young girl in the film was a prostitute who needed the money. Mrs. Carter says, "I'd never have married you if I'd known. Never" (*CS*, 358). Carter, however, is caught up in his memory of the girl to whom he made love in the film and confesses he loved her. Mrs. Carter cannot believe he could have loved a tart, but he assures her that he had.

When they return to their apartment, Carter locks himself in the bathroom and prays to God that his wife be dead when he reenters the room so that he will not have to endure her insults. But she has actually been stimulated by the blue film and makes love to Carter for the first time in years. Greene describes her in terms of a bird of prey, a creature he always feared: "Her thin bare legs reminded him of a heron waiting for a fish" and, in the midst of the sex act, "she screamed like an angry and hurt bird" (*CS*, 360). Carter's final thought is that "he had betrayed that night the only woman he loved" (*CS*, 360).

In the topsy-turvy world of this story true love is found outside of marriage (which is almost always the case in Greene's novels), for only there can Greene's heroes find sexual fulfillment. In many cases Greene portrays the females who satisfy his sexually frustrated heroes as coming from the lower class in the third world. Carter's sense of betrayal carries a social and political implication. In his miserable sexual encounter with his wife he has betrayed the white man's burden.

In "Special Duties" (1954) Greene satirizes the Catholic doctrine of indulgences. Devout Catholics believe that by saying prayers or performing certain rituals they may gain for themselves or for others the remission of purgatorial punishment that remains after their sins have been forgiven in the sacrament of penance. The mechanical, bookkeeping aspect of this practice had made it an object of satire since the time of Chaucer.

Greene's story focuses upon William Ferraro, an Italian Catholic and wealthy London businessman. His wife, who believes herself to be an invalid, lives in a separate wing of their great house. Because she chooses to live each day as if it will be her last, she has a priest reside in the wing with an emergency bell in his room. Greene's brief sketch of Mrs. Ferraro reads like a parody of Vivien's intense religious beliefs, which contributed to her emotional and, finally, physical isolation from her husband.

Mr. Ferraro is also concerned about his death but, being a busy man of the world, he hires a personal secretary, a 30-year-old woman named Miss Saunders, and assigns her the special duties of accumulating indulgences for him. She seems well qualified for the job, for she had been the head girl at a convent school where she won the special prize for piety for three consecutive years. During her three years employment she has apparently managed to amass 36,892 days of released time from Purgatory for Mr. Ferraro.

But one day Mr. Ferraro decides to visit a church in Canon Wood where, Miss Saunders has informed him, she was going in order to gain him a 60-day indulgence. He discovers there is no such church in the neighborhood and has his chauffeur drive him to the home of his secretary in a seedy section of London. From his car he happens to catch sight of her at her window. He is startled to see her scantily clad. The hot weather, he thinks, at first, but then he sees a man's arm encircle her waist and next a hand pull the curtain across the window.

After his discovery of Miss Saunders's deception, Mr. Ferraro suddenly seems to age and is oppressed by thoughts of death: "He sat down in a chair and a slight pain in his chest reminded him of his double pneumonia. He was three years nearer death when Miss Saunders was appointed first" (*CS*, 354). Knowing comedy to be the best defense against the idea of death, Greene has his hero conclude the story with an appropriate thought: "Tomorrow I will set about getting a really reliable secretary" (*CS*, 354).

Greene employs parody and comedy in this story as a means of dealing with some of his serious concerns and experiences. As already mentioned, the story includes the theme of marital separation: the religious reclusive wife versus the practical man of the world. Then, as a Catholic convert, Greene was faced with a system of beliefs that all too easily can degenerate into false piety. Over and again in his novels Greene depicts his pious Catholics (such as Ryker in *A Burnt-Out Case*) as sentimental, cruel, and unforgiving. Unlike Greene's other pious characters, however, Miss Saunders really harms no one. We do not judge her harshly because the discovery of her hypocrisy (temporarily) undermines the foolish religiosity of Mr. Ferraro. Finally, like Mr. Ferraro, Greene had to confront his own mortality when his doctors told him he might have lung cancer. A bronchoscopy, however, revealed his chest pains were caused by double pneumonia. This terrifying memory is anesthetized through the comic deferral of death and salvation Mr. Ferraro announces at the story's conclusion. Later, in "Under the Garden," Greene revises the memory of his fatal diagnosis to motivate his hero, Wilditch, to revisit the place of his childhood.

A Sense of Reality

Greene's next collection of short fiction, *A Sense of Reality* (1963), contained only four stories: "Under the Garden," "A Visit to Morin," "Dream of a Strange Land," and "A Discovery in the Woods." The focus in these stories, however, is upon dreams, myth, and the imagination, not upon reality. The ironic title of the collection reflects an important theme Greene was developing about this time: the inseparability of fiction and reality.[16] In *Our Man in Havana* (1958) Greene comically played with the notion that an author may be able to create real-life characters. In "Under the Garden" Greene has his hero, Wilditch, boldly assert that "Absolute reality belongs to dreams and not to life" (*CS*, 224). And so the title *A Sense of Reality* echoes Wilditch's insight and sets forth the theme that an author's version of reality, drawn from his subconscious and his dreams and embodied in his narrative, is his only reality: his fiction is his *sense* of reality. As Brian Thomas has noted, "The organizing thematic principle in this sequence of four stories is that reality becomes intelligible only to the extent that it yields to some more-or-less coherent narrative view of it."[17]

By the addition of three stories ("Church Militant," "Dear Dr. Falkenheim," and "The Blessing") to "A Sense of Reality" in the *Collected Edition*, Greene weakens the unifying theme of the volume. These added stories not only ignore myth and dreams, they shift the tone of the collection from one of serious self-analysis to one of light satire.

"Under the Garden" is Greene's longest (about 23,000 words) and most ambitious story, one that self-consciously mythologizes his fears, obsessions, dreams, and fascinations. The complex structure of this story reflects the labyrinthine ways that the narrator, William Wilditch, must travel in his quest for self-discovery.

Wordsworth's notion that the child is father of the man is a helpful one in understanding the theme of this story. The restless and unhappy adult, confronted with his own mortality and unable to see a purpose or significance to his life, by reliving a powerful childhood dream discovers his hidden self—the imaginative child within him—and so finds illumination, meaning, and fulfillment. Greene gives an ironic twist to the recurrent theme of Victorian novelists (especially Dickens), whose heroes search for their biological or symbolic fathers, by having his hero set out on a quest for his lost childhood. In finding his childhood under the dreamlike garden Wilditch paradoxically discovers his symbolic father.

"Under the Garden" is a fairy tale embodied in a dream vision that the narrator, William Wilditch, experiences upon returning to the house where he spent his childhood summers. Wilditch feels compelled to revisit Winton Hall, now in the possession of his brother, after his doctors inform him that he has a fatal obstruction in his lungs. He begins to reflect upon the relationship between the child and the man: "Now the dreaming child was dying of the same disease as the man. He was so different from the child that it was odd to think the child would not outlive him and go on to quite a different destiny" (*CS*, 174).

Wilditch's mother stands in opposition to his romantic dreams. He says he really never knew her very well and his brother explains that she "had very decided views . . . about any mysteries, and that turned her against the garden. Too much shrubbery, she said. She wanted everything to be very clear. Early Fabian training, I daresay" (*CS*, 177). Greene's own mother, Marion, was also a remote figure, someone who could not show her feelings toward her children and who relied upon her practical sense and intellect to deal with her family. In short, she was the perfect foil for the imaginative child who had to keep his fantasies hidden from his rational mother.

The setting for Wilditch's dream is an island in the lake near Winton Hall. He remembers a great adventure he had there as a child and is disappointed at first to discover that the lake is only a shallow pond and the island not much larger than the top of a kitchen table. Nevertheless, he believes that as a child he spent three days and nights below the ground out there and refuses to accept his brother's recollection that he was there only a few hours.

He reads a story he wrote as a child about his adventures underground and is disappointed to find that the account does not match his memory of the dream. The real adventure did not involve pieces of eight, Spanish galleons, and crucifixes. It was much more surrealistic and radical. He thinks he must have falsified his adventure in order to avoid the criticism of his mother, that he wrote a "cover story" to protect himself. Reflecting Greene's belief in the significance of dreams as narratives of reality, Wilditch says, "Of course it had all been a dream, it could have been nothing else but a dream, but a dream too was an experience, the images of a dream had their own integrity, and he felt professional anger at this false report" (*CS*, 185). In part 2 Greene shifts the point of view from omniscient to first person as Wilditch writes out the truthful version of his bizarre adventures under the garden.

Greene's interest in Lewis Carroll reveals itself throughout the story. Wilditch was Alice's age, seven, when he first ventured underground through a cavelike arch in the roots of a great tree. As he proceeds deeper into the earth he discovers a timeless world ruled by a paradoxical figure named Javitt and his grotesque wife, Maria. As will be seen later, Javitt expresses a *Wonderland* philosophy of life based upon paradox, irony, intimidation, and linguistic playfulness. His bullying, know-it-all style recalls such *Wonderland* and *Looking-Glass* characters as the Caterpillar, the Hatter, and Humpty Dumpty, all of whom engage Alice in dazzling conversations filled with threats, illuminations, mystery, and challenging dicta. Like Carroll, Greene finally restores Wilditch to the real world and leaves him with an ambiguous symbol of his underground adventure, an old tin chamber pot. In his dream vision the pot was pure gold. At the conclusion of *Alice's Adventures in Wonderland* Alice is not sure if she is dreaming of the Red King or if she is a figure in the dream of the Red King. Fiction and reality are also blended in the conclusion of *Through the Looking-Glass*, where Alice is shaking the Red Queen, who turns into Alice's kitten as Alice wakes from her dream.

Javitt, who sits on a toilet seat like a king on a throne, embodies the intuitive and creative energy of the underworld. A big old man with a white beard, he is a composite of a Blakean god, an Old Testament Prophet, and a dirty, vulgar old man. Young Wilditch says he reminds him of a monarch, a prophet, "the gardener my mother disliked" (*CS*, 202), and a policeman in the next village. He is a twinned personality who paradoxically reconciles the sublime and the vulgar, the transcendental and the excremental, romance and disillusionment, childhood and experience. As Wilditch observes, despite his coarse, rustic speech, Javitt's "ideas seemed to move on a deeper level, like roots spreading below a layer of compost" (*CS*, 202).

Javitt's very name, which conjures up the names "Yahweh" and "Jehovah," suggests his authority in the underworld. He makes clear, however, that Javitt is not his real name: " 'You can call me Javitt,' he said, 'but only because it's not my real name. You don't believe I'd give you that do you? . . . 'If you had a dog named Jupiter, you wouldn't believe he was really Jupiter, would you?' " (*CS*, 203). Like the Hebrew god, Javitt's true name is ineffable. His comment about the name of the dog, however, raises the interesting philosophic subject of the relationship of names (words) to things (reality). Again, Lewis Carroll provides the model for Greene in this linguistic adventure. In *Through the Looking-Glass* Humpty Dumpty explains to Alice that names must mean something and that his name designates his shape. With a name like Alice, he observes, she could be almost any shape.

Greene is fascinated with the mystery of the inner person, "the man within" as he called him in an early novel, and extends the idea in *A Burnt-Out Case*, in which the hero has the significant name of Querry. Like Javitt, Querry's sense of self cannot be comprehended by outsiders: they merely form fictional versions of him.

The underground world presents both an excremental and a transcendental vision to the hero. The god of the underworld sits upon a toilet, the air has "an odd disagreeable smell like cabbage cooking" (*CS*, 192), and Wilditch complains to Javitt, "I couldn't stay here with you. It's not—sanitary. . . . I'd die" (*CS*, 201). When Javitt offers to show him a picture of his beautiful daughter—"I'll show you something which will give you dreams" (*CS*, 207)—Wilditch's need to relieve himself becomes urgent and Maria fetches him a golden potty. The daughter, with the comic name of Miss Ramsgate, has gone "upstairs" as Javitt says, and, upon looking at her picture, Wilditch swears he will never marry anybody but her. She becomes the idealized object of his quest for romance and sexual fulfillment. When he exclaims he is going to find her when he gets out of the earth, Javitt cautions him, "you'd have to live a very long time and travel a very long way to find her" (*CS*, 219). Wilditch thus acquires his dream vision of transcendental love out of the excremental underground world. Out of the sordid bodies of Javitt and Maria comes the spiritual beauty of Miss Ramsgate. Yeats noted the paradox years earlier when, in "Crazy Jane Talks with the Bishop," he wrote, "Love has pitched his mansion in / The place of excrement."

Maria is not only ugly, she is grotesque. Having no roof to her mouth, the only sound she can make is a birdlike "Kwahk." Greene, who was always afraid of birds, describes Maria's hands as "curved like a bird's," her nails filled with dirt. Her hair is gray and straggly and she is going bald on top. In short, she represents Greene's childhood nightmare image of the witch at the corner of his nursery he knew would one day grab him. She is a version of Mrs. Baines from "The Basement Room." Unlike her husband, who rules her, she is inarticulate and powerless to harm the young boy, but as the grotesque embodiment of the Earth Mother, she has given birth to beauty. Greene acknowledges that out of his nightmares come the obsessive quests for idealized dreams, one of the fundamental paradoxes realized in the story.

Javitt expresses the major paradox of "Under the Garden" when he explains to Wilditch that "Absolute reality belongs to dreams and not to life" (*CS*, 224). This is the great lesson Wilditch discovers now that he is faced with death from lung cancer. His return to Winton Hall and his childhood dreams are not so much an escape from reality as an escape to the greater reality of the imagination and the beautiful narratives woven out of childhood memories. Wilditch's doctors may work to save his body, but Javitt is the true savior, the child-father who lives deep within Wilditch's subconscious mind, who, once discovered, blesses the fears and disorders of life with startling significance.

After Wilditch completes writing his recollections of his dream, he finds on the island an old tin chamber pot that shows only a few flakes of yellow paint. This common and vulgar household object is a tangible symbol of his rediscovered self and carries him away from the world of decay and disillusionment back to the "golden po" brought to him underground 50 years ago when he first saw the photograph of the most beautiful girl in the world. Previous to his visit to Winton Hall, he told his doctors he was not sure he wanted to prolong his sort of life: "I have no curiosity at all about the future" (*CS*, 170). Greene describes Wilditch's renewed mental state, as he sits with the battered potty between his legs, with a surprising and appropriate simile: "He had a sense that there was a decision he had to make all over again. Curiosity was growing inside him like the cancer" (*CS*, 236–37).

"Church Militant" (1956) originally appeared in the Catholic periodical *Commonweal*, whose liberal Catholic readers would enjoy Greene's satiric and down-to-earth depiction of the clergy. The story is set in Kenya shortly after the British troops had driven the Mau Mau, a terrorist, antiwhite organization of Kikuyu tribesmen, into the forest mountains. Although the story is a comic one, the setting provides a dangerous backdrop against which the foibles of the priests and nuns who live near the Kikuyu reserve can be assessed.

The satire is aimed at a group of idealistic, European nuns, the Little Sisters of Charles de Foucauld, who have come to Kenya to realize their dream of living like African women on Kikuyu ground. The archbishop ignores the protests of his fellow priests that this place is unsuitable for women, despite the fact that only recently several bodies were found with their throats cut. The archbishop simply replies, "It's their vocation, father, it's their vocation. You are too materialist" (*CS*, 270).

This is not an especially funny or memorable story, but it reveals Greene's skill at capturing personalities within a short space. The nuns, interestingly, never actually appear in the story. These invisible pious women and the authoritarian archbishop are stock characters who never come alive. Fathers Donnell and Schmidt, however, are more realistically drawn figures. Like the characters in "M*A*S*H," they thrive on practical jokes in the midst of bloody warfare.

First published in the *London Magazine* in 1957, "A Visit to Morin" sets forth Greene's paradoxical credo as a Catholic writer. The narrator, a wine merchant named Dunlop (Greene's family wealth was derived from wine), has admired the Catholic novels of Pierre Morin ever since he was a schoolboy. Although he is a Protestant, Dunlop had a Roman Catholic teacher who introduced him to the writings of Morin. Although he is now fading into obscurity, Morin once offended orthodox Catholics in his own country of France and pleased liberal Catholics abroad (Greene himself enjoyed a similar reputation, his novels being acclaimed by liberal French Catholics such as François Mauriac). As a boy Dunlop viewed Morin as a revolutionary writer. He notes that Morin was accused of being a Jansenist and that his characters carry their ideas to extreme lengths (charges that critics have leveled against Greene's own writings).

Years later, while on a business trip to Colmar, Dunlop discovers that his boyhood hero lives nearby. Driven by curiosity and perhaps the hope of discovering some spiritual certainty, he searches for Morin and finds him at the Christmas Eve celebration of midnight Mass. He wonders why this distinguished Catholic does not join the others in receiving Holy Communion. After Mass Dunlop introduces himself, and the author then invites him to his home where, under the influence of several brandies, he reveals his paradoxical faith to the narrator.

Morin explains that he lost his belief in God over 20 years ago but has never relinquished his faith. He argues that his "lack of belief is a final proof that the Church is right and the faith is true" (*CS*, 254–55) and the reason he does not return to the sacraments is his fear that his belief would not be restored: "As long as I keep away from the sacraments, my lack of belief is an argument for the Church" (*CS*, 255).

By belief Greene means an approach to God through formal theology and institutional ritual and dogma. Faith, on the other hand, represents a personal acceptance of God's love. Years after he wrote this story

Greene, speaking of himself, said: "There's a difference between faith and belief. If I don't believe in X or Y, faith intervenes, telling me that I'm wrong not to believe. Faith is above belief. One can say that it's a gift of God, while belief is not. Belief is founded on reason. On the whole I keep my faith while enduring long periods of disbelief."[18]

Morin's (and Greene's) casuistical logic is a good example of what Dunlop noted earlier, namely, that Morin's characters carry their ideas to extreme lengths. Of course, Morin, as a self-reflexive character in Greene's narrative, properly reflects his creator's enjoyment in testing the border between orthodox and radical theology. Morin echoes Greene's position on the subject of faith when he attacks the scholastic arguments for the existence of God and says, "I would prefer the thoughts of an ape. Its instincts are less corrupted. Show me a gorilla praying and I might believe again" (*CS*, 251).

This story also deals with the dynamic relationship between fiction and reality and the ironic contrasts between public and personal perceptions. Morin tells Dunlop that "Perhaps I wrote away my belief like the young man writes away his love. Only it took longer—twenty years and fifteen books" (*CS*, 252). With the protective hedge of a "perhaps," Greene enunciates here the romantic notion that an author sacrifices his soul in his writings. The man and his work become one but, paradoxically, the man who remains in time, outside of the work, is a hollow, depleted, sacrificial figure. His audience, however, confuses the actual man with his fictional counterpart. Morin says to Dunlop, "You must realize that I wouldn't speak to any one of my neighbours as I have spoken to you. I am their Catholic author, you see. Their Academician. I never wanted to help anyone believe, but God knows I wouldn't take a hand in robbing them . . ." (*CS*, 252). There are mirrors within mirrors operating here. Through Morin's confidential disclosure to Dunlop of his loss of belief, Greene manages to broadcast his own disillusionment to millions of his pious readers.

Like Morin, Greene experienced the public's confusion of his fiction with his personal life. He received numerous letters, especially from women and priests, requesting his counsel about their marital or religious problems. He was hounded for years by the religious public, leading him to write, "I felt myself used and exhausted by the victims of religion."[19] A few years later Greene used the theme of "A Visit to Morin" as the basis for his novel *A Burnt-Out Case* (1961). Critics interpreted the novel, as they did the short story, as autobiography. Greene's response to the critics is interesting: "If people are so impetuous as to regard this book as a recantation of faith I cannot help it. Perhaps they will be surprised to see me at Mass" (*Ways*, 229). One wonders if Greene was aware of the irony of this remark: it was at Mass that Dunlop discovered the unbelieving Morin. In his autobiography, as in his fiction, Greene remains a character in an ongoing narrative he employs in order to gain his own sense of reality.

Set in Sweden, "Dream of a Strange Land" (1963) is the story of a man who has contracted leprosy while in Africa and is anxious to receive private treatment for his disease in order to avoid having his life made even more miserable through public disclosure of his illness at a hospital. The old professor of medicine who has been treating him now says he can no longer continue to do so and the patient must enter a hospital. Shortly after the patient leaves, the professor's house is transformed into a gambling casino for one night in order to entertain a senile general. When the leper returns that evening to make a final plea for treatment, he discovers the bizarre metamorphosis of the house: "The patient stood motionless in the snow, with his face pressed to the glass, and he thought, The wrong house? But this is not the wrong house; it is the wrong country. He felt that he could never find his way home from here—it was too far away" (*CS*, 295). When the champagne corks are popped amid the celebration within the house, a faint explosion is heard outside the house; the leper has apparently committed suicide.

Reminiscent of Querry in *A Burnt-Out Case*, the patient is the familiar Greene outcast looking in on a society that seems fabricated, unreal, and one he knows he can never join. "His "home" is as far away and unreachable as Querry's dream of a peaceful land, and only death will bring an end to his suffering.

The relationship between the doctor and his patient is the familiar one of victim and betrayer. As Brian Thomas has observed, "the ultimate revelation of 'Dream of a Strange Land' is that the betrayer of the story is perceived as lost too: the inset narrative turns the leprologist into the same kind of stranger and victim as his patient, so that each becomes the mirror image or double of the other" (105). After the patient commits suicide the doctor looks at the window where "he thought a moment ago that someone looked in as lost as himself, but no one was there" (*CS*, 297).

Even when Greene sets his story in the distant future, as in "A Discovery in the Woods" (1963), he asserts the familiar theme of lost innocence. This story offers an account of an isolated race of small, deformed people living after an atomic blast. A group of children explore the woods around their village and discover the remains of a large boat on top of a hill, and in it a skeleton. One of the boys looks down on his own stunted and uneven legs, and the girl next to him begins to "keen again for a whole world lost" (*CS*, 323). The boy marvels at the discovery lying at their feet: "He's six feet tall and he has beautiful straight legs" (*CS*, 323). As in "The Basement Room" the adults are the villains who warp the sensibilities of the young. This time the adults have destroyed the secret garden of childhood with the ultimate weapons of destruction instead of with lies and secrets.

The favorite game of the children is called "Old Noh," which reflects Greene's theme that myth and reality are intertwined. Through the game the children transform the reality of their painful inheritance of dwarfed, crippled bodies, caused by the ignorance and atomic violence of their ancestors, into a Noah myth of a lost golden age of beautiful giants. They thus survive a morbid, shattered reality through their shared belief in a mythic past.

"Dear Dr. Falkenheim" (1963) is written in the form of a letter by a man concerned about his son's childhood trauma to a psychiatrist named Dr. Falkenheim. The narrator arouses the reader's curiosity by withholding the traumatic event until near the end of his account. He begins by recording the details of his family's vacation in Canada, a place he finds an exciting contrast to his home in England. He and his wife are well educated and determined to raise their six-year-old son, Colin, according to enlightened psychological methods. Their main concern is to wean Colin from his belief in Father Christmas, but when they learn that a large department store is going to fly Father Christmas by helicopter into the shopping center they decide to allow Colin one last year of fantasy.

The helicopter carrying Father Christmas arrives and as it hovers over the heads of the excited spectators he opens his sack and drops hundreds of small bright packages. When the helicopter finally lands, however, and Father Christmas makes his dramatic exit, he accidentally walks into the slashing blades. Greene's description of the scene is notably vivid and grotesque: "The blades took his body and flung it in a kind of violent dance back the way he had come and his head was sliced right off and spun through the air, white detachable beard and all, and it landed a dozen paces away with open eyes and a look of amazement before the body had time to topple out of its dance" (*CS*, 279).

The narrator reveals the irony of the boy's trauma in the final paragraph of his letter. Now 12 years old, Colin is the butt of his contemporaries' practical jokes every Christmas because he firmly believes Father Christmas really existed: "'Of course he's real,' he says, a bit like an early Christian, 'I saw him die'" (*CS*, 280). The father concludes his letter: "He's dead, and so he's indestructible. Please do what you can, Doctor . . ." (*CS*, 280).

On first reading, this story may appear simply as a playful foray into black humor, but its theme arises out of Greene's own deep and painful sense of childhood disillusionment. Comedy and irony are his means of defending himself against the relentless memory. By casting the story in the form of a letter to a psychiatrist, Greene is recalling his own experience in recording and disclosing the details of his psychic traumas to the psychoanalyst Kenneth Richmond. By depicting in grotesque detail the decapitation of Father Christmas, the symbol of childhood innocence and trust, Greene suggests the unforgettable psychological violence he underwent in losing his own naive beliefs in heroes, love, and loyalty. The ironic conclusion is a clever defense against the acceptance of loss and conjures up the mythic dimension of the story. The phrase "like an early Christian" suggests that Colin thinks in a manner similar to Christ's followers who mythologized his death and resurrection.

"The Blessing," which was published in both the *New Statesman* and *Harpers* in 1966, is perhaps the weakest addition to the expanded version of *A Sense of Reality* in the *Collected Edition*. It is the story of a journalist named Weld, who works for a popular London newspaper. He has been assigned to cover the Archbishop's blessing of army tanks about to be sent off to war against the Germans. Sympathetic with the pacifist movement, Weld is naturally critical of the sanctification of weapons of death, but he talks to an old peasant man who instructs him in the paradoxical nature of a true blessing. The old man explains that "we have to bless what we hate. . . . I've never known a blessing to save a life. But then, if you want to bless, you bless. It would be better to love, but that's not always possible" (*CS*, 263). Later, when a fellow journalist says to Weld that he loves whisky as much as the Archbishop loves his dear old tanks, Weld replies, "You don't bless what you love." The other journalist then asks, "What about your cigarettes then?" Weld's response concludes the story: "They are my enemy. They'll kill me in the end. . . . I've never known a blessing save a life" (*CS*, 264).

May We Borrow Your Husband?
and Other Comedies of the Sexual Life

The 12 stories that comprise *May We Borrow Your Husband? and Other Comedies of the Sexual Life* (1967) were written, according to Greene, "in a single mood of sad hilarity, while I was establishing a home in a two-roomed apartment over the port in Antibes" (*CS*, x). The setting for many of the stories is Antibes, and the narrator is often an observant writer who, like Greene, eavesdrops on the conversations he hears in his favorite restaurant:

> Taking my dinner nightly, in the little restaurant of Felix au Port, some of the tales emerged from conversations at other tables (even from a phrase misunderstood), though the title story had been in my mind for a number of years. I had brought the idea with me to Antibes as part of my baggage, and I set the scene in Antibes, though in fact I had seen the incident happen under my eyes (or so I imagined) at St. Jean-Cap Ferrat while I worked at a hotel window on a very different subject, *A Burnt-Out Case*. (*CS*, x)

Unlike the stories in the previous collections, those in *May We Borrow Your Husband?* are nearly all comic. Some of Greene's novels, such as *A Burnt-Out Case* (1961), *The Comedians* (1966), and *The Honorary Consul* (1973) exhibit his sense of irony and black humor, but only in this collection of stories and in two novels and two plays (*Our Man in Havana*, 1958; *Travels with My Aunt*, 1969; *The Complaisant Lover*, 1959; *The Return of A. J. Raffles*, 1975) does he successfully express the manic side of his manic-depressive personality. Even his light comedy, however, is a facet of his essentially melancholy view of life. As he himself notes, "perhaps the stories which make up the collection *May We Borrow Your Husband?* . . . are an escape in humour from the thought of death—this time of certain death. Writing is a form of therapy; sometimes I wonder how all those who do not write, compose or paint can manage to escape the madness, the melancholia, the panic fear which is inherent in the human situation" (*CS*, xii).

The earliest story in this collection is "A Shocking Accident," which originally appeared in *Punch* in 1957. The comedy of this story has nothing to do with sexuality but derives from a slapstick piece of black humor. Young Jerome, a student at an expensive preparatory school, is called into the office of Mr. Wordsworth, the housemaster, to be given bad news about his father. Jerome worshipped his father and in imagination has transformed the widowed author into a mysterious adventurer. He has come to believe that his father is in the British Secret Service or is a gunrunner and thinks that he must have been wounded in a hail of machine-gun bullets. Mr. Wordsworth, suppressing his laughter, explains that "Nobody shot him, Jerome. A pig fell on him. . . . Your father was walking along a street in Naples when a pig fell on him. A shocking accident" (*CS*, 111). It seems that in the poorer section of Naples the people keep pigs on their balconies. This pig, which was on the fifth floor, had apparently grown too fat, the balcony broke away, and the pig fell upon the boy's father and killed him. Jerome's startling response to this news is "What happened to the pig?" (*CS*, 112).

Years pass and Jerome becomes engaged to a girl named Sally. He is not sure if his love for her would continue were she to laugh at the story of his beloved father's death but he knows she eventually must be told. One evening Jerome's aunt tells the story and "then the miracle happened. Sally did not laugh" (*CS*, 117). Jerome is elated when she expresses horror at the awful accident and later asks, "Penny for your thoughts, my darling." She replies, "I was wondering what happened to the poor pig?" (*CS*, 117). "They almost certainly had it for dinner," Jerome says and kisses Sally again.

Greene maintains a delicate balance between pathos and bathos in this hilarious story. Less accessible to critical analysis, Greene's comedy is nevertheless an essential component of his vision of life. This story, *Our Man in Havana*, and *Monsignor Quixote* reveal a comic genius that has never been fully realized or appreciated. Greene's obsession with such subjects as lost childhood, failure, pity, hatred, the isolated and hunted man, betrayal, suicide, dreams, seedy and decadent surroundings, violence, and carnal sexuality dominates his fiction and obscures his sense of the absurd and of the comic twists in life.

"Awful When You Think of It" (1957) originally appeared in *Punch* in the same year as the preceding story. Both tales exhibit the light tone and droll sense of humor appropriate to that magazine. What makes this story unusual is that it treats the serious subject of lost childhood innocence in a comic manner. The humor functions as a defense against the romantic brooding that this subject usually arouses in Greene.

The narrator announces his theme at the outset: "It is awful how little we change" (*CS*, 124). Echoing Wordsworth's line, "The child is father of the man," he says. "Even as a baby we carry the future with us" (*CS*, 124). He explains it has always been his hobby "to visualize in a baby's face the man he is to become—the bar-lounger, the gadabout, the frequenter of fashionable weddings; you need only supply the cloth cap, the grey topper, the uniform of the sad, smug or hilarious future" (*CS*, 124).

The rest of the story is an imagined dialogue that the narrator has during a railway trip with a baby temporarily left in his care by its mother. The narrator's imagination transforms the baby's grunts, grins, and laughter into a civilized chat as if between two men in a pub discussing the stock market and exchanging funny stories.

Beneath the comic surface of this story Greene is asking the solemn question posed by Yeats in "Among School Children": "What youthful mother, a shape upon her lap . . . / Would think her son, did she but see that shape / With sixty or more winters on its head, / A compensation for the pang of his birth, / Or the uncertainty of his setting forth?" To be sure, the imagined adult version of the baby in this story is not a suicidal, dislocated, brooding figure like Scobie in *The Heart of the Matter* or Querry in *A Burnt-Out Case,* but is depicted as an ordinary, dull mortal who ironically asserts his identity by becoming a member of a fashionable club where he offers "Doubles all round." The club may refer to the shared adulthood of the narrator and his imagined companion, and "doubles" may suggest the narrator sees his own unhappy twin in the grown child.

"May We Borrow Your Husband?" (1962), the title story, is narrated by a fictional version of the author. Like Greene, William Harris is a writer staying in Antibes while working on a biography of the earl of Rochester. Greene, in fact, published a biography of the earl in 1974, entitled *Lord Rochester's Monkey.* This detail is significant because it reveals the narrator to be predisposed to explore the wit and sexuality that surrounds him in Antibes. Rochester was notorious for his witty, polished, and licentious poetry, not to mention his reckless sexual behavior. His religious conversion late in life must also have appealed to Greene.

The story deals with two homosexual interior decorators, Tony and

Stephen, who attempt to seduce a young man away from his bride during the couple's honeymoon. They manipulate the narrator to entertain the bride, Poopy (to whom he is attracted, despite his age), while they drive off with her husband, Peter. At the end of the story Poopy naively announces that Tony will visit them in London for several months in order to decorate their house.

The narrator depicts the two homosexuals, Tony and Stephen, as cruel, witty, and self-indulgent creatures who hunt their prey with the cunning of animals. On the other hand, he, himself, comes across more as a voyeur than as an interested spectator. He records in obsessive detail the sexual comedy that develops around him. His research on Rochester parallels and is informed by his research into the lives of Tony and Stephen, Poopy and Peter. He cannot substantially change the course of Rochester's life, but he is tempted to intervene in the present comic scene in order to keep it from turning tragic. When he first sees Peter and Poopy approaching the hotel he thinks: "I had a wild impulse to lean over the balcony and warn them away—'Not this hotel. Any hotel but this'" (*CS*, 9). Afraid to be thought an eccentric, he allows the farce to begin and later becomes a participant in it as it moves toward a seemingly inevitable and unhappy conclusion. "This was the first time I wanted to interfere," he says, "and I didn't know them at all. The second time it was already too late, but I think I shall always regret that I did not give way to that madness" (*CS*, 9–10).

Greene legitimizes his narrator's interest in the private lives of those around him by having him become an actor in the tragicomedy. Harris self-consciously addresses the reader: "You will notice that I play a very unheroic part in this comedy. . . . There was no move I could make. I had just to sit there and watch while they [Stephen and Tony] made the moves carefully and adroitly towards the climax" (*CS*, 24). Recognizing Harris's interest in Poopy, Tony and Stephen offer her to him while they borrow her husband for a trip to an adjacent village.

When the narrator is alone with Poopy he is strongly tempted to tell her to go back home, that she has married a man whose only interest is in other men and that he is now picnicking with his boyfriends. Her innocence and vulnerability, however, keep him silent. Waiting for her to explain her unhappiness, he views her situation in the only terms that make sense to him, those of fiction: "It was a little like a novel which hesitates on the verge between comedy and tragedy. If she recognized the situation it would be a tragedy; if she were ignorant it was a comedy, even a farce—a situation between an immature girl too innocent to understand and a man too old to have the courage to explain" (*CS*, 31). When she finally tells him that Peter has not made proper love to her since their arrival in Antibes, that he starts but never finishes, Harris again validates her complaint with a literary parallel— "Rochester wrote about that" (*CS*, 31)—as if that somehow made sense of the problem. As she proceeds to disclose the intimate details of her frustrated sexual life with Peter, the narrator confesses "I was finding now that I really wanted her" (*CS*, 32). His scruples, however, keep him from taking advantage of her.

Peter spends the night and most of the next day with his boyfriends, leaving the 50-year-old Harris to enjoy another day of playing father confessor and potential lover to Poopy. When the three men return, Tony explains to Harris that "le pauvre petit Pierre" had convinced himself he was impotent: "Poor Poopy. She just hadn't known the right way to go about things. My dear, he has a superb virility" (*CS*, 39).

The next morning Poopy tells Harris that now everything is all right, Peter truly loves her, and Tony plans to come to London to decorate their house. Seeing through the deception, Harris is tempted to intervene and save Poopy from unhappiness but he again assumes the passive role of the novelist, content to record the details of this sexual comedy. He rationalizes, "But I was just as bad for her as he [Peter] was. If he had the wrong hormones, I had the wrong age" (*CS*, 42).

There is not much healthy, robust, or romantic sexuality in Greene's fiction. Rather, Greene seems to express a disgust for sex. Mabel Warren, an alcoholic lesbian journalist in *Stamboul Train*, is depicted as self-indulgent and vicious. Pinkie Brown in *Brighton Rock* is a profoundly repressed young man who displaces his sexuality into brutal violence. Greene's fiction is also filled with unhappy adulterers and older men who fall in love with young girls. "May We Borrow Your Husband?" embodies several of these sexual misfits: homosexuals and the older man sexually aroused by the pathos and innocence of a young woman.

In "Beauty" (1963) Greene reverts to one of the themes of "Under the Garden," namely, the paradoxical relationship between beauty and ugliness, as he again draws together the aesthetic and the excremental views of his subject. Greene's projection of his dark, seedy, and sordid vision upon the world of his novels has led critics to name that psychological territory "Greeneland." In addition to Greeneland, however, one must recognize its opposite but equally important territory: dreamland. Like the romantic poets, out of whose work many of his themes derive, Greene is driven by ideals, dreams of a more perfect place, the alluring simplicity of childhood, peace, and immortal beauty. And like the romantic poets, he recognized that these ideals were enhanced by their opposites: the fallen world of violence, fear, ugliness, and death. Thus the beautiful Miss Ramsgate in "Under the Garden" is the child of the grotesque Maria and her shockingly vulgar husband who reigns from his seat on a toilet. Thus the pathetic, mutilated leper Deo Gratias in *A Burnt-Out Case* seeks a mystical place of wholeness and joy remembered from his childhood.

Beauty is the spoiled and pampered Pekinese of a self-indulgent old woman who builds her life around her dog. The narrator says, "I think he was the most perfect Pekinese I have ever seen" (*CS*, 44). The dog's beauty is enhanced by the various metaphors the narrator lavishes upon its description, elevating the creature to the level of a symbolic embodiment of aesthetic beauty: "He would have been as white as milk if a little coffee had not been added, but that was hardly an imperfection—it enhanced its beauty." His eyes "seemed deep black like the centre of a flower" (*CS*, 44). His owner explains to a friend that she could not possibly visit them in London because Beauty would have to be locked in "a horrible prison" where he certainly would pick up a disease.

Having established the unsullied beauty of the dog in the first part of the story—as well as its owner's implicit perversion in treating the animal with the smothering intensity of a possessive mother—Greene then deflates the image of the idealized beauty by depicting the dog's nasty bestial instincts. While walking down the narrow, dirty, back streets of Antibes the narrator discovers Beauty climbing into a garbage can, discarding old fruit skins, rotten figs, and fish-heads, until he gets hold of a long tube of some animal's intestines: "he tossed it in the air, so that it curled round the milk-white throat. Then he abandoned the dustbin, and he galumphed down the street like a harlequin, trailing behind him the intestine which might have been a string of sausages" (*CS*, 47).

Greene appears to relish describing moments of disillusionment. In "Dear Dr. Falkenheim" he animates the decapitation scene by having Father Christmas's headless body move "in a kind of violent dance" (*CS*, 279). In "Beauty" he calls upon Lewis Carroll's comic word "galumphing" to depict the dog's playful expression of his unbridled instincts. Greene's final description of the dog's fall from aesthetic grace, however, is even more grotesque. The dog discovers some excrement on the pavement and begins to roll its body over it: "He tested the ordure first, like the clubman he was, with his nostrils, and then he rolled lavishly back on it, paws in the air, rubbing the *cafe-au-lait* fur in the dark shampoo, the intestines trailing from his mouth, while the satin eyes gazed impertubably up at the great black Midi sky" (*CS*, 47). The story ends with the dog's owner pathetically calling to it out the window and the narrator thinking, "if it had not been for that hideous orange toque, I would have felt some pity for the old sterile thing, perched up there, calling for lost Beauty" (*CS*, 47).

The title of the story "Mortmain" (1963) comes from the legal world and refers to the transfer of property to a corporate body for perpetual ownership. The irony of the title gradually reveals itself. After living 10 tormented years with his mistress, Josephine, Carter, at age 42, marries a compassionate and understanding woman named Julia and looks forward to years of marital bliss. Josephine, however, continues to enter his home during the following months whenever the couple is away and leaves seemingly pleasant notes hidden around the house. Her happy notes and favors (such as lighting their fireplace so that they can be warm together upon their return from Athens) are actually sinister attempts to undermine Carter's marriage. Josephine has not transferred her emotional property, Carter, for perpetual ownership by her rival.

Another irony in the story is that Julia continues to defend Josephine to her husband. She recognizes a truth in Josephine's note that says, "I feel we have so much in common, having loved the same man" (*CS*, 69). As the notes continue to show up in such places as under their mattress, however, Carter becomes so distressed that he begins searching for notes throughout the house and attacks Julia for failing to see Josephine's sinister plot to destroy their marriage.

Greene's decision to name his hero Carter is significant because it is the name of his hated classmate in Berkhamsted, Lionel Carter. Carter's torment of the young Greene is avenged in this story by Josephine's sinister and sophisticated harassment of the fictional Carter. Julia's continued defense of Josephine is rather hard to believe and seems contrived to reinforce the revenge motif. Although Josephine is an artistic designer by profession, Greene works out her vengeance through her writing, making his identification with her more forceful. A writer by profession, Carter ironically becomes a victim in the sinister drama written and staged by his mistress.

"The Root of All Evil" (1964), one of Greene's most sustained farces, asserts the theme that secrecy leads to lies, drunkenness, fornication, scandal, murder, and subornation of authority. Set in Germany, the story contains a double narrative. The narrator recounts a story told him by his severe, Protestant father. Intended as a moral lesson about the evil of secrecy, the father's story concerns a small group of men who decide to meet and drink in secret in order to avoid the deadly company of the boring Herr Puckler. Puckler's curiosity concerning the whereabouts of his fellows grows to paranoid proportions. He involves the police in the search for their meeting place and argues that they must be secretly working to undermine the government.

The chief farcical technique in the story is transvestism. As Herr Schmidt attempts to lead Puckler on a false trail, Schmidt enters a brothel he mistakes for an inn. After taking his pleasure there he sees a policeman who is waiting outside. In order to help Schmidt escape from the house, the women dress him like a peasant woman.

Later in the story Greene pushes the comedy of female impersonation to an extreme. Puckler dresses in a woman's clothes in order to get hired as a cook for the secret-club members, thereby allowing him to spy on their activities. He is subsequently joined by a policeman, also dressed in a woman's clothes, to assist him in his surveillance on the suspected anarchists. Meanwhile, the men of the club learn of the deception and attack the two spies in a grand slapstick finale. Puckler's head is crammed into a chamber pot and by the time it can be removed he is dead.

The narrator concludes his father's story—with its stern pronouncements upon the evil of secrecy—with a clever irony. He recollects his father's rising to the climax of his moral outrage and saying, "Men in women's clothes—the terrible sin of Sodom." "And what's that?" his son asks. "At your age," his father replies, "some things must remain secret" (*CS*, 151).

Greene's finest story in this collection is "Cheap in August" (1964), a surprisingly tender and compassionate tale in light of the cruelty and superficiality in the stories that surround it. An Englishwoman named Mary Watson is on vacation in Jamaica because it is "cheap in August." Although she loves her American husband, an English professor, at home working on a study of James Thomson's "The Seasons," she decides she wants to have an affair, an adventure. She quickly discovers, however, "the essential morality of a holiday resort in the cheap season; there were no opportunities for infidelity, only for writing postcards" (*CS*, 82).

Thirty-nine years old, she feels it is absurd not to be content, but her restlessness is not due simply to physical desires, she argues, but represents "the universal desire to see a bit further, before one surrendered to old age and the blank certitude of death" (*CS*, 86). As fate would have it, she is soon involved in the most unlikely, bizarre affair, one she never planned but that profoundly affects her life.

At the swimming pool she meets an American named Henry Hickslaughter. Greene describes him as "a solitary elephant," an old man with "rolls of fat folding over the blue bathing-slip" (*CS*, 88). They have lunch together, and before long Mary begins to feel oddly at ease with the old man. In a way, Henry is like herself. He too came to Jamaica because it is cheap in August, and he appears lonely and unfulfilled, and with little time in life remaining to find happiness. That evening she goes to his room for a drink, and they discuss a variety of subjects, from Longfellow to their family lives. They then go down for dinner, after which he invites her back to his room because, as he says, "I don't sleep well." She refuses at first, afraid that perhaps even at his age Henry might have some sexual designs on her. These thoughts make her feel ignoble, however, and she feels unjustified in refusing him a half hour's companionship; and so she goes to his room with a bottle of sleeping pills to help him sleep.

When she enters the room she is startled to find him crying. "I wanted company," he says, and she reassures him. He admits he is afraid of being alone and would have paid the maid to stay with him if necessary. At this point Henry is no longer described as an elephant but as a geographical region to be explored and marveled at: "It was as if she were discovering for the first time the interior of the enormous continent on which she had elected to live" (*CS*, 107). The stereotypical American turns out to have a tender soul, scarred by failure and dread. "But here, stretched on the bed . . . failure and fear talked to her without shame, and in an American accent. It was as though she were living in the remote future, after God knew what catastrophe" (*CS*, 107).

Like an anxious and troubled child soothed by his mother, Henry finally falls asleep. Mary lies on the bed beside him outside the sheet, and he is lying away from her so their bodies do not touch. But filled with pity and compassion she arouses his sexuality, and they make love. She feels no guilt but weeps a little at the temporary nature of this meeting. And when "His body began to slip out of her, . . . it was as if he were carrying away her unknown child, in the direction of Curaçao, and she tried to hold him back, the fat old frightened man whom she almost loved" (*CS*, 108–9).

Greene's description of Henry in geographical terms of an unexplored America is especially poignant in light of Mary's marriage to Charlie, a proper Bostonian. Prior to meeting Henry, her knowledge of America was shaped by Charlie, books, and motion pictures: "There had been no mystery anywhere from Miami to Niagara Falls, from Cape Cod to the Pacific Palisades. . . . Nobody anywhere admitted failure or fear; they were like sins 'hushed up'—worse perhaps than sin, for sins have glamour—they were bad taste" (*CS*, 107). Charlie has substituted an abstract, literary America for the real thing. As a professor and writer he is able to provide a critical and intellectual narrative about American literature but has lost touch with the human needs of his wife. Conditioned by his puritanical heritage, his literary studies ignore the vulnerability, fears, and failures that drive the lives of people around him. Charlie's next book will be called *The Double Reflection*, a study of the influence of Fenimore Cooper upon the European scene. The title carries a subtle irony in the story, for his double, Henry Hickslaughter, has an enormous impact upon Charlie's European wife.

On one level this story makes one think of Henry as Greene himself, in need of a loving younger woman to reassure and comfort him in a terrifyingly impersonal world. Over and over again Greene has presented heroes, such as Fowler in *The Quiet American*, Scobie in *The Heart of the Matter*, and Castle in *The Human Factor*, with similar needs. There is also an ironic sense of sexuality and motherhood fused in the women of these works. The men are old enough to be fathers to their women but they frequently present themselves as frightened children who need these females to comfort and nurture them.

There is a wonderful innocence about Henry. The fact that he is an American is important, for Greene has previously presented Americans as innocents but not as sympathetic ones. The Smiths in *The Comedians* are well-meaning fools and Alden Pyle in *The Quiet American* is unthinkingly cruel, but Henry Hickslaughter, despite his name, is depicted as a vulnerable, failed human being in need of love and compassion. He is the lost child seeking a home and never really finding it, except for the brief encounter in Jamaica. He is the unknown child who irrevocably slips away from Mary. She has discovered America and lost it in the same night.

Greene's attitude toward sexuality may have been shaped by his father. As headmaster of Berkhamsted School, Charles Greene was determined to inculcate manliness in his boys. A devout Christian, he was ruthless in maintaining the moral tone of the school. He dismissed boys caught kissing girls or masturbating. After he found one boy lounging about with his hands in his pockets, he ordered the boy's pockets to be sewn up. The greatest evil, however, was homosexuality, a perversion Charles Greene could neither understand nor abide.

Anthony Nichols, who was a student at Berkhamsted when Charles Greene was headmaster, recalls the man's bewilderment by sex and his awkward interrogations of suspected students. Greene would ask a boy, "Do you know what masturbation is?" or "How many times have you masturbated?" When the boy recovered from his intimidation, Greene would shout, "You boy, you will go, go, get out of my sight" (quoted in Sherry 1989–, 1:43). Graham Greene himself recalls being questioned by his father to see if he was a victim of a suspected masturbation ring. Greene writes that his father "found the situation beyond him—perhaps he even believed the popular fable of his generation that masturbation led to madness" (*Sort*, 81).

In his story "Doctor Crombie" (1965), set in a boy's school named Bankstead (an obvious reference to Berkhamsted), Greene parodies his father's campaign against sexuality through his depiction of the eccentric school physician, Doctor Crombie. The narrator, reflecting upon his early school years, recalls Doctor Crombie addressing the assembly of boys on the subject of personal hygiene and informing them that masturbation causes cancer. Some years later he meets Doctor Crombie again, who tells him that he has been asked to resign from the school. His dismissal has not been caused by his bizarre theory about masturbation causing cancer, but by his claim that prolonged sexual relations also cause cancer, even in a proper marriage. The children's parents readily tolerated the former caution, but the latter touched too directly on their own lives and they have demanded Crombie's removal.

Since he has fallen in love with a girl and now also has a personal stake in the matter, the narrator eagerly questions the old man about the subject. Crombie points out that "Almost one-hundred percent of those who die of cancer have practised sex" (*CS*, 134) and that he himself lives alone and has never been greatly tempted by sex. Connecting his weird theory with that of evolution, he concludes that "the natural processes of evolution see to it that an animal becomes extinct when it makes a wrong accidental deviation. Man will perhaps follow the dinosaur" (*CS*, 135).

In the final paragraph the narrator reveals that Doctor Crombie died quietly one night of pneumonia. Now past 60, the narrator explains he was led to think of Doctor Crombie when his physician told him he had lung cancer: "My sexual desires . . . are beginning to diminish, and I am quite content to follow the dinosaurs into obscurity. Of course the doctors attribute the disease to my heavy indulgence in cigarettes, but it amuses me all the same to believe with Doctor Crombie that it has been caused by excesses of a more agreeable nature" (*CS*, 135).

Through this clever and amusing tale Greene is able to resurrect his father's eccentricities and hallow them with good humor and sympathy. Despite Doctor Crombie's peculiarities, he maintains a vigorous integrity in the face of ridicule and his dismissal from his post.

"The Over-Night Bag" (1965) is a grim comedy about a little gray man named Henry Cooper and the secret contents of his BOAC flight bag. During his flight from France to his home in London he goes to unusual lengths to protect his bag from being crushed by the luggage of the woman sitting next to him. She becomes annoyed at his strange behavior (he fastens the bag with a seat belt) and asks him what it contains. "A dead baby," he says. "I thought I had told you" (*CS*, 59). He tells her that it is not his baby, but his wife's, and casually continues reading his magazine.

After Henry passes through Customs, he takes a taxi to his apartment, which he shares with his mother. He asks the taxi driver to turn down the heat because he does not want the dead baby in his bag to deteriorate. Unlike the woman passenger who was outraged by Henry's actions, the taxi driver accepts the bizarre story in a matter-of-fact and comical way. He assures Henry that babies keep a long time, longer than old people, and keeps referring to the baby as a "little perisher" (*CS*, 61). When Henry explains that he intends to take the dead baby home for the night and see about arrangements the next day, the taxi driver says, "A little perisher like that would fit easily into the frig. No bigger than a chicken. As a precaution only" (*CS*, 62).

When he gets to his apartment, he finds that his mother has laid out his slippers in front of his armchair and has changed the position of his favorite picture so that she does not have to see it from her chair. It is a reproduction of a painting by Hieronymus Bosch. She asks him if he made any new friends and he replies that wherever he went he made new friends. She then asks if he has had any adventures and he says he found a little toe in his marmalade. The dialogue is surrealistic:

> "It wasn't English marmalade?"
> "No, Mother, foreign."
> "I could have understood a finger—an accident slicing the orange—but a toe!"
> "As I understand it," Henry Cooper said, "in those parts they use a kind of guillotine worked by the bare foot of a peasant."
> "You complained, of course?"
> "Not in words, but I put the toe very conspicuously at the edge of the plate." (*CS*, 63–64)

The story closes with Henry's mother going into the kitchen to put a shepherd's pie into the oven and with Henry going down the hall to fetch his flight bag. "Time to unpack," he thinks. "He had a tidy mind" (*CS*, 64), the narrator remarks, concluding the tale.

The interpretation of this story, of course, is left to the curious reader. Greene raises more questions in this tale than he is willing to answer. Henry may simply be doing what he claims: carrying his wife's dead baby home for burial. But where is his wife? And why does he live with his mother? What does he mean when he says that it is not *his* baby, but his wife's? Is the baby illegitimate? Did he murder it?

A less melodramatic way of reading this tale is to see Henry as a lonely eccentric, someone who has never escaped his mother's domination. His adventures are those of the imagination. Never married and carrying nothing interesting in his flight bag, he makes up stories to shock those around him and to give meaning to his own dreary reality. Henry's grotesque imagination is validated by the painting by Bosch, an artist renowned for his nightmarish and violent monsters. The story about the dismembered toe Henry found in his marmalade and discreetly put to the side of his dish is in keeping with this same bizarre version of reality.

The overnight bag, then, may simply be the bag of tricks of Greene, the fictional conjurer. By engaging our curiosity about the contents of the bag and the implications of those contents, he is establishing a central thesis in his work: a fictional narrative is the most significant version of reality available to us. We can never know reality, only a fictional version of it. As readers we must fill the overnight bag with meaning even as an author validates his own meaning through his writing.

Like several of the earlier stories in this volume, "The Invisible Japanese Gentlemen" is about the writer's art. The narrator, a writer hardly distinguishable from Greene, reports the conversation he over-hears between a young woman about to have her first novel published and her apprehensive fiancé. The story works out two strategies simulta-neously. The reported conversation reveals the young woman to be superficial and unobservant while, at the same time, the narrator's slice of life, filled with relevant details of character and setting, shows him to be a keen observer and an accomplished writer. Greene draws the satiric portrait of the deficient budding author—with its ironic conclusion—with a sense of superiority inherent in his very style.

The opening paragraph illustrates Greene's Holmesian dedication to the powers of observation: "There were eight Japanese gentlemen having a fish dinner at Bentley's. They spoke to each other rarely in their incomprehensible tongue, but always with a courteous smile and often with a small bow. All but one of them wore glasses. Sometimes the pretty girl who sat in the window beyond gave them a passing glance, but her own problem seemed too serious for her to pay real attention to anyone in the world except herself and her companion" (*CS*, 118). In only four sentences Greene introduces all of the characters in his story, the setting, the ethnic identification of the foreign diners, their number, what they are eating, their manner, how many of them wore eyeglasses, the attractiveness and seating location of the young woman, and her self-centeredness.

The young woman, in contrast, although she glances at the party of Japanese men several times throughout the meal, is too blinded by the romance of her literary future to actually see them. When her fiancé questions the title she has chosen for her next novel, *The Azure Blue*, by remarking, "I thought azure *was* blue" (*CS*, 121), she looks at him with disappointment and informs him her editor said she was a born novelist with remarkable powers of observation. When she and her fiancé are leaving the restaurant, he asks, "I wonder what all these Japanese are doing here?" Her reply provides the narrator with his climactic observation of her doomed literary future: " 'Japanese?' she said. 'What Japanese, darling? Sometimes you are so evasive I think you don't want to marry me at all' " (*CS*, 123).

In the process of the story the narrator acknowledges his own failure to go beyond his initial observation of this couple. When he first sees them he describes them as matching works of art: "She had thin blonde hair and her face was pretty and *petite* in a Regency way, oval like a miniature. . . . [her] fiancé resembled her physically. I could see them as two miniatures hanging side by side on white wood panels. He should have been a young officer in Nelson's navy in the days when a certain weakness and sensitivity were no bar to promotion" (*CS*, 118–19). By the end of the story, however, the narrator comes to realize they are fundamentally mismatched: "Her Regency counterpart, I suppose, would have borne a dozen children without the aid of anesthetics, while he would have fallen an easy victim to the first dark eyes in Naples" (*CS*, 122). The narrator secretly hopes her first novel is a failure and that she take up photographic modeling while he establishes himself securely in the wine trade.

In "Chagrin in Three Parts" (1966) Greene returns to the subject of homosexuality. The title has a double meaning: the story is told in three parts and each of the three main characters (the narrator, Madame Dejoie, and Madame Volet) feels chagrin for past mistakes in love or for wasted opportunities. Unlike the cutting and judgmental portraits of homosexuals in *Stamboul Train* and "May We Borrow Your Husband?," the lesbian lovers in this story are allotted a small degree of sympathy and humanity. Nevertheless, a compelling sense of desperation pervades the atmosphere of the story from its outset, and Greene's depiction of Madame Dejoie occasionally bristles with hostility.

The writer-narrator opens his story with a description of Antibes in February. The tourists have all gone home, it is raining, the statues are "emaciated," the masts of the ships in the harbor are bare, and the stores and restaurants are closed for the season, with the exception of Felix au Port, where the narrator discovers the subject for his story. The desolate setting establishes the psychological atmosphere of emptiness and abandonment experienced by the three characters seeking to regain lost love.

The narrator's first impression of Madame Dejoie is an adversarial one. As he approaches the restaurant he sees her staring out at him through the window. A very powerful lady dressed in black, she looked as though she were willing him not to enter: "she regarded me with too evident distaste. My raincoat was shabby and my shoes were muddy and in any case I was a man" (*CS*, 48). He watches her hand clutch a huge peppermill "like a bludgeon" (*CS*, 49). Like Tony and Stephen in "May We Borrow Your Husband?," she is depicted as aggressive, domineering, arrogant, clever, and exploitative.

When Madame Volet arrives, the narrator is surprised at how attractive she is and listens with great interest to the story of her husband's cheating on her. Madame Dejoie tries to comfort her by telling her that she too lost a beloved husband. The narrator's detail that her husband died from a disease of the bowels recalls Greene's delight in juxtaposing excremental and romantic images.

As the two women continue to talk, Madame Dejoie reveals her self-centeredness, her insatiable desires, and her cleverness in securing her next lover: "I adored my husband . . . yet it was only after his death I discovered my capacity for love. With Pauline. You never knew Pauline. She died five years ago. I loved her more than I ever loved Jacques, and yet I felt no despair when she died. I knew that it was not the end, for I knew by then my capacity" (*CS*, 54). When Madame Volet confides that she has never loved a woman, Madame Dejoie exclaims, "*Cherie*, then you do not know what love can mean. With a woman you do not have to be content with *une facon classique* three times a day" (*CS*, 54). And as they continue to get drunk together, Madame Dejoie attacks male sexuality: "When you really think of it, how comic that little object is. Hardly enough to crow about, one would think. . . . Perhaps smoked like an eel one might enjoy it" (*CS*, 55). The narrator shows remarkable restraint in concluding this section of the story with the comment: "They were drunk, of course, but in the most charming way" (*CS*, 55).

Like the narrator of "May We Borrow Your Husband?," the narrator of this tale is tempted to become a character in his own story: "like most of my fellow writers I have the spirit of a voyeur—and I wondered how stupid married men could be. I was temporarily free, and I very much wanted to console her" (*CS*, 50). In this triangle, however, he remains passive and begrudgingly leaves the pleasure of consoling to his competitor, Madame Dejoie. At the end of the story, when the two tipsy women leave the restaurant together, Madame Volet gives a hop and a skip and throws her arms around Madame Dejoie's neck. The narrator, sitting alone in the restaurant, concludes his story on a bittersweet note: "I was glad she was happy again. I was glad that she was in the kind reliable hands of Madame Dejoie. What a fool Paul [Madame Volet's husband] had been, I reflected, feeling chagrin myself now for so many wasted opportunities" (*CS*, 56).

There may be considerable irony in the sentence about the "kind reliable hands of Madame Dejoie." Throughout the story Greene depicts her as a powerful and willful individual. Only after the two women become drunk, more relaxed, and vulnerable does the narrator display any regard for Madame Dejoie. She is, after all, the main actor in this little drama. She makes things happen, unlike the narrator, who continues to dip into his Trollope novel during the meal. Captivated by the real-life story unfolding in front of him, however, he abandons his novel in order to create a fictional record of another comedy of the sexual life.

Told from the point of view of an omniscient observer, "Two Gentle People" (1967) also develops the theme of lost opportunities. In the course of an afternoon a middle-aged man and woman, both of whom are married, meet for the first time, develop a friendship, have dinner together, and, on the brink of starting a love affair, return to their unhappy married lives.

The story opens on an idyllic afternoon in a French park. Marie-Clair, an attractive French woman, and Henry Greaves, an American expatriate, are enjoying the last warming rays of the sun when a passing teenager maliciously kicks and wounds one of the pigeons nearby. Driven by pity for the suffering bird, Henry quickly wrings its neck. Through that dramatic moment of violence and compassion Greene brings his two characters closer together.

Henry and Marie-Claire discreetly begin to open their lives to each other. She tells him she was too cowardly to kill the bird and that she admires him for his courage and pity. Her remark leads him to begin a confession of his own cowardice, but sensing an unwarranted revelation, she changes the subject. Henry apparently was going to disclose his cowardly attitude toward his wife, his fear of trying to break out of a miserable marriage. Both Marie-Claire and Henry have childless marriages and both sense they are missing an essential happiness and meaning in their lives.

Their coming together in this chance manner, their brief touching of minds and desires, conveys a fatalistic melancholy into their day: "the hour had come too late in both their lives" (*CS*, 159). The narrator observes, "What is cowardice in the young is wisdom in the old, but all the same one can be ashamed of wisdom" (*CS*, 159).

In the final two scenes of the story, showing Marie-Claire and Henry returning to their spouses, Greene underscores the personal misery that brought this couple to the brink of happiness and new chances. Marie-Claire goes straight to her room, knowing that her husband has taken a new male lover, and through the wall she hears their sexual frolic. Finally she stuffs beads of wax into her ears and dreams "how different things might have been if fifteen years ago she had sat on a bench in the Parc Morceau, watching a man with pity killing a pigeon" (*CS*, 160). Henry returns to his nagging, neurotic wife (ironically named Patience), who accuses him of visiting the park to pick up young girls.

Greene does not portray Patience very convincingly. He resorts to a stereotype of the vulgar American, showing her to be addicted to Coca-Cola, cigarettes, bitching, and sex. Greene's anti-Americanism is tempered in the case of Henry Greaves, however, because he is an expatriate, a Jamesian character, redeemed by his European tastes and refined sensibilities.

One of the most pleasant treats afforded by the stories in *May We Borrow Your Husband?* is the insight they give us into the writer's mind and imagination. We witness the narrator, as eavesdropper and voyeur, discovering and creating characters and weaving plots and counterplots out of the scraps of conversation he picks up in restaurants and hotels. Occasionally, as in the title story, "May We Borrow Your Husband?," he becomes a character in his own tale. The more curious among us can identify with the narrator, for how many times have we not, like him, attempted to flesh out the fragments of conversations we have overheard in public places in an attempt to reconstruct a meaningful story about interesting strangers who might otherwise simply pass through our lives without notice, like those invisible Japanese gentlemen.

The Last Word

The Last Word (1990) represents Greene's "last word" as a writer of short fiction, and as such conveys a synoptic view of the stages of his life as a writer. Many of the stories, in fact, resemble sketches of atmosphere or character preliminary to the novels or memoirs he was writing at the time.

The first story, "The New House" (1923), written during his undergraduate days at Oxford University, is one of his first stories to discard the heavy-handed trappings of allegory and melodrama for a realistic portrayal of an idealist being corrupted by money. (This story is fully examined in the earlier section "Loosing the Devils.") "Murder for the Wrong Reason" (1929) reflects Greene's interest in the dual personality, a subject he explores in greater detail in his retracted novel *The Man Within*, published the same year. "The Lottery Ticket" (1938) shows Greene's engagement with the politics and violence of Mexico and anticipates his more comprehensive vision of that land in *The Power and the Glory*. "The News in English" (1940) and "The Lieutenant Died Last" (1940) reflect Greene's patriotism and interest in espionage during the war. "Work Not in Progress" (1955) and "The Man Who Stole the Eiffel Tower" (1956) display his whimsical mode during the time he was writing his comic masterpiece, *Our Man in Havana*. "An Appointment with the General" (1982) is a section of a novel abandoned in favor of a book-length memoir, *Getting to Know the General* (1984). Reminiscent of the melancholy comedy of the stories in *May We Borrow Your Husband?*, "The Moment of Truth" (1988) reflects the 83-year-old Greene's thoughts about death. "The Last Word" (1988) is also about death, but the melancholy and loneliness of the preceding story is here replaced with a strong Christian faith that welcomes death as a release from a futuristic godless world. In "An Old Man's Memory" (1989) Greene all but abandons the pretense of fiction to assume again the role of a Jeremiah, predicting on a smaller scale this time, not the end of Christianity, but the destruction of the Channel Tunnel. Finally, in "A Branch of the Service" (1990), a story published for the first time, Greene reverts to the comic style of *Our Man in Havana* in depicting the absurdities involved in undercover operations.

"Murder for the Wrong Reason" appeared in three installments in the *Graphic* in October 1929. Although Greene disparages and wishes he had suppressed his first published (though third-written) novel, *The Man Within* (1929), he has seen fit, after 60 years, to reprint the short story he wrote at the same time, a story that embodies the theme of the divided self he also explores in his novel. The editor of the *Graphic* prefaces the story with the following comment: "The young author of this story of murder with an unusual twist in its detection won an instantaneous success this year with his first novel, *The Man Within*, and a brilliant future is predicted for him."[20]

Unlike the rather straightforward stories he wrote during his years at Oxford, "Murder for the Wrong Reason" is overwritten, complex, and dependent upon a surprise ending. It is a story that requires at least two readings before one can feel confident about understanding it. The manner in which the story was originally presented in the *Graphic*, with synopses of each preceding installment and with illustrations of the various characters, significantly shaped the readers' expectations and understanding of the action. Both the synopses and the illustrations create, as will be discussed shortly, plentiful red herrings that lead one to misread the story and to have to backtrack.

Here is the synopsis that appears at the beginning of the third installment:

> Detective Inspector Mason, entering the offices of Hubert Collinson with a search warrant, finds the body of its owner huddled in the swivel chair, with a knife in the heart. Mason telephones to Scotland Yard, and also summons a constable from a neighbouring beat. He tells the constable that Collinson had been a blackmailer. Together they search for clues while awaiting the arrival of an able detective from the Yard. The constable finds a letter to the dead man signed "Arthur Callum." Mason says he knows Callum, who actually lives quite near. The constable, with visions of rapid promotion, asks his superior if they cannot pay a quick visit to Callum's flat before the arrival of the fast car from Scotland Yard. The Inspector re-reads the letter, and confronts Callum in the latter's flat. After fruitlessly interrogating him Mason leaves the flat, and on the stairs meets Rachel Mann, an ambitious actress who had become Collinson's mistress, though Callum had loved her and asked her to marry him. He tells her that the tragedy was her doing and goes into a reverie of

the past. Returning to the scene of the crime he tells the constable that Callum is not the man they want, but promises him a spectacular triumph, saying that the air is full of clues. . . .[21]

Among the five illustrations that accompany the story is a depiction of Mason's confrontation of Callum that shows the two men to be distinctly different. There is also an illustration of Mason's meeting with Rachel Mann outside Callum's flat. At the end of the story, however, the reader discovers that Rachel Mann has been dead for 10 years and that Mason's meeting with Callum and Mann occurs only in his mind and that Callum is, in fact, Mason's youthful alter-ego and not an actual character in the story. Both the synopsis and the illustrations, therefore, are red herrings designed to trick the reader, leaving him feeling cheated at the conclusion of the story.

In the final installment Greene reveals that Mason is himself the murderer. Mason melodramatically offers himself up for arrest by the constable, assuring the latter of his promotion. In retrospect, one realizes that Mason not only committed the murder but that he also set up the constable to "discover" the clues. Like Arthur Conan Doyle, Greene has Mason create the mystery and then urge the constable to solve it.

Mason/Callum could have killed Collinson years before "for the right reason"—jealousy over a woman. As it stands, he killed Collinson for "the wrong reason." As he says to the constable, "You don't see a jealous lover here, constable, only an elderly, corrupt police officer who has killed his blackmailer."[22] Greene never makes clear why Collinson was blackmailing Mason nor how Rachel Mann died. At the beginning of the story Mason declares that " 'Collinson deserved all that he got. Blackmail,' he added, 'and women' " (*Last Word*, 113). Clearly Mason's dealings with Collinson have involved these two separate issues, and the blackmail may have been about women, or a woman, or the death of a woman.

One of the ways in which Greene deals with the theme of the split personality is through the symbolism of a painting depicting the resurrection of Lazarus from the dead that hangs on the wall of Mason's/Callum's flat. The painting also appears in one of the illustrations. Mentioned several times throughout the story, the painting suggests the resurrection of Mason's dead, youthful self. Mason frequently speaks of his "private inquiries," which suggests not only his investigation into the crime but, more significantly, his introspective dialogues, his encounters with the man within. It may be that this interesting psychological subtext combined with an experimental detective story explains Greene's decision to include the story in this collection. Reading the story more than 60 years after he wrote it, Greene comments: "I found that I couldn't detect the murderer before he was disclosed. During those early years in the twenties and thirties I was much interested in the detective story (I even began *Brighton Rock* expecting it to be a detective story)" (*Last Word*, viii).

During the winter of 1938 Greene spent five weeks in Mexico to undertake research for a book about the Mexican Revolution. Mexico was a dangerous country to visit at the time, for President Plutarco Elias Calles, in the name of his socialist revolution, was closing down the churches and exiling or murdering priests and practicing Catholics. Greene's brief visits, nevertheless, yielded three significant works: "The Lottery Ticket" (1938), a short story, *The Lawless Roads* (1939), an account of his travels through Chiapas and Tabasco, and *The Power and the Glory* (1940), one of his finest novels.

"The Lottery Ticket," though written in 1938, was not published until 1947, when it appeared in the *Strand Magazine* and *Cosmopolitan*. It was also included in Greene's collection, *Nineteen Stories*, which was published in England that same year. Curiously, Greene omitted the story from the American version of *Nineteen Stories* (1949) and from subsequent collections of his short fiction until the publication of *The Last Word* in 1990. Greene explains that he excluded the story from his earlier collection because "I thought then that there were too many echoes in it of *The Lawless Roads* and *The Power and the Glory*. Well, those two books today belong to an even more distant past, so I decided to give 'The Lottery Ticket' a second chance" (*Last Word*, vii–viii).

Many of the details of setting and character in "The Lottery Ticket" are, indeed, reflected in *The Power and the Glory*: the seedy, derelict atmosphere of the Mexican towns, the omnipresent vultures waiting for another death, the roaches on the hotel walls, the banana plantations, the dentist, the fat chief of police preaching social progress, and the themes of fatalism and betrayal. Despite the evocative character of Mexico Greene develops in this story, it cannot compete with the fully realized character of the land he conjures in his novel.

Greene does not handle point of view in "The Lottery Ticket" with his usual skill. The story is basically told by an omniscient author. Nevertheless, Greene opens his tale with a first-person narrator who soon gives way to the omniscient author. After introducing Mr. Thriplow, an Englishman on holiday in Mexico who has just purchased a lottery ticket, the narrator comments, "I don't often believe in fate, but when I do I picture it as just such a malicious and humorous personality as would choose, out of all people in the world, Mr. Thriplow to fulfill its absurd and august purposes" (*Last Word*, 80). There is no indication who this narrator is, and after the opening paragraph he simply recounts Mr. Thriplow's adventures.

Shortly after his arrival in a dirty and depressing village, Mr. Thriplow learns he has purchased a winning lottery ticket worth 50,000 pesos. Enjoying comfortable circumstances in England, he does not really need the money and feels ashamed at having won the lottery in the midst of so much Mexican poverty. To overcome the guilt of being a foreign exploiter and gringo, he goes to a bank and offers the money to the manager so that some good might be done with it locally. Perhaps the money could be used to establish a free library or a hospital. As he becomes involved with the Governor and the Chief of Police, however, Mr. Thriplow discovers his money will be used to "defeat reaction" (*Last Word*, 88).

The Mexican state's view of social progress turns out to be quite different from that of Mr. Thriplow, whose British liberalism and naïveté lead to ironic consequences. It appears the money he turns over to the government is used to pay the wages of the police and the military. When Thriplow sees the government soldiers moving down the street to arrest another of the Mexican patriots, a defender of the church, he rushes to the rebel's house to warn him. The man's daughter answers the door and the dialogue that follows carries Greene's attack upon foolish British liberalism:

> "It was you who gave the money, wasn't it?"
> "It was, but you understand . . . no personal feeling. I am a Liberal. I cannot help sympathising with . . . progress."
> "Oh, yes."
> "I detest Fascism. I cannot understand how a patriot—I am sure your father is a patriot—could take arms from Germany, Italy . . ."
> "What a lot you believe," she said with faint derision. (*Last Word*, 93)

She then reveals to him that the soldiers have already carried off her father, presumably for execution.

This simple woman, a former nun, exhibits a political savvy and human understanding that overwhelms Thriplow in his moment of bitter disillusionment. Determined to make the affair easy for him, she asks for some money to help bury her father, saying, "You have done your best for us. You could go home quite happy. . . . I can see you are a kind man. Only ignorant . . . of life, I mean" (*Last Word*, 95). With his innocence devastated, Thriplow's feelings turned to hate "for all who had so unexpectedly broken into his life, hate of the new ideas, new words. Hate increased its boundaries in his heart like an annexing army. . . . and hate spread across Mr. Thriplow's Liberal conscious-ness, ignoring boundaries. . . . It seemed to Mr. Thriplow . . . that it was the whole condition of human life that he had begun to hate" (*Last Word*, 95).

Like *The Power and the Glory*, this story has its clear-cut villains—the Chief of Police, the Governor, and the military—and its heroes—the executed patriot and his daughter. What complicates this story is the focus upon Mr. Thriplow. His presence diffuses the tension that should arise from the opposition between the government and the rebels, the hunters and the hunted, and shifts the reader's attention to his disillusionment. The damaged feelings of a British liberal on holiday in Mexico thus becomes more significant than the political and human fate of a nation and the Catholic church. Perhaps here is another reason why the story disappeared from the American edition of *Nineteen Stories* and failed to appear in subsequent collections until 1990.

Greene published two short stories during the war, "The Lieutenant Died Last" and "The News in English," both of which show the British to be courageous opponents of the Germans. These tales might be read as simple morale boosters, as Greene's literary contribution to the war effort. He explains that he excluded them from *Collected Stories* not because he found them unworthy but because "Time (and with it Memory) passes with horrifying speed. How many people below the age of sixty would remember Lord Haw-Haw, whom I listened to nightly in 1940 on the radio, and understand the title and subject of 'The News in English'? In that war, they might well ask, was it plausible for a squad of foreign soldiers to descend by parachute on an English village? None had occurred in the German war and we had been engaged in at least three conflicts since then. The questions are even more relevant today than in 1967, but I am taking the risk of reprinting them because I like the stories" (*Last Word*, vii). For those under 60, Lord Haw-Haw was an Anglo-American named William

Joyce who broadcast German propaganda in English from Berlin during the Second World War. He was captured by British soldiers in Germany in 1945, convicted of treason, and hanged.

"The Lieutenant Died Last," published in *Collier's* in 1940, is a whimsical tale about German parachute troops attacking an English village. While out poaching rabbits on Lord Drew's grounds in the small village of Potter, Bill Purves sees a small group of Germans parachute onto the field. While some of the soldiers round up the villagers and imprison them in the local tavern, Bill Purves engages the others in a gun battle and kills or wounds them. He then returns to the tavern, where the soldiers stationed there, seeing that Purves is armed, surrender to him. The narrator's conclusion to this tale displays a British pride and patriotism with a comic touch and a laconic hero. Despite his heroism, Purves is charged with poaching: "He was quite gratified: he didn't expect medals and as he said, 'I've got one back on them bloody Bojers'" (*Last Word*, 58).

An action-filled and humorous story, "The Lieutenant Died Last" also contains a brief note of seriousness. The wounded German lieutenant calls out to Purves to kill him. The narrator comments that "Old Purves always felt pity for broken animals, but he hadn't a bullet left." He then picks up the officer's revolver and kills him. Afterward he looks through the dead man's pockets and discovers a photograph of a naked baby on a hearthrug. His sense of humanity, suppressed during his battle with the Germans, overcomes him and he becomes sick to his stomach. Purves keeps this souvenir of his encounter with the Germans but never shows it to anyone. "Sometimes he took it out of a drawer and looked at it himself—uneasily. It made him—for no reason that he could understand—feel bad" (*Last Word*, 59). The theme of pity, which became an obsessive one for Greene in his later works, surfaces even here, in this comic salute to British patriotism, and demonstrates that in Greene's mind pity transcends national boundaries.

"The News in English," published in the *Strand Magazine* in 1940, is one of Greene's earliest tales of espionage. Unlike his later spy novels, such as *Our Man in Havana* (1958), which satirizes the British Secret Service, and *The Human Factor* (1978), which makes a hero of a British traitor, "The News in English" celebrates the heroic patriotism of a British double agent.

Set during the Second World War, the story opens with Mrs. Bishop and her daughter-in-law, Mary, listening to a radio broadcast from Germany. The voice they hear on the radio is that of a typical English don who is proclaiming the resurgence of youth throughout the new Germany. Mrs. Bishop recognizes the voice as that of David, her son and Mary's husband. A mathematics don at Oxford, David was reported in the newspapers to have gone to Germany to evade military service, leaving his wife and mother to be bombed in England. At the time, Mary fought in vain with reporters, arguing that David must have been forced to leave England. Mrs. Bishop, however, condemns her son for his cowardice and betrayal while Mary persists in her attempt to make sense of his bizarre actions.

One evening during his broadcast David announces that somewhere back in England his wife may be listening to him: "I am a stranger to the rest of you, but she knows that I am not in the habit of lying. . . . The fact of the matter is . . ." (*Last Word*, 21–22). At that moment Mary suddenly realizes that her husband is speaking to her in code. When he was away from her on trips he employed a scheme whereby the phrase "the fact of the matter is" always meant "this is all lies, but take the initial letters which follow" (*Last Word*, 23). Mary discovers that David is sending her details of Germany's military secrets.

Reporting this information to the War Office, Mary is told to keep David's subterfuge secret, even from his mother, otherwise his and many other lives will be lost. The War Office agrees to broadcast a message using the same code to Germany in the hope that David will hear it. The message explains how he can obtain a safe passage home.

Meanwhile, Mary must silently endure her mother-in-law's contempt for David. On his final broadcast, after reporting some military secrets, he says goodbye to his wife, indicating to her that he never received the War Office's message and that he is now lost to her forever. Mrs. Bishop exacerbates Mary's pain by commenting, "He ought never to have been born. I never wanted him. The coward," driving Mary to cry out, "if only he were a coward, if only he were. But he's a hero, a damned hero, a hero, a hero . . ." (*Last Word*, 31). Mary is left with an agonizing truth that she cannot reveal and looks to a future time when she can restore her husband's good reputation.

The painful note on which this story ends anticipates the conclusion of *The Human Factor*, where Castle, the British defector living in Russia, telephones his wife in England, knowing he will never be able to see her again. Castle's motivations for spying are complex and involve his loyalty to the Communists for helping to get his wife, a South African, out of her country. One of the problems with "The News in English" is that Greene fails to establish any motivation for

David's presence in Germany. Since the War Office had no knowledge of his coded messages until Mary reported to them, David could not have been an official double agent. One can only assume that the newspaper reporters were right, that he left England to avoid military service. Once there, however, his conscience presumably led him to join the war effort by spying on the German military and hoping that his wife remembered their childish code. The story, unfortunately, does not make this very clear.

Lying behind the patriotism of this tale is Greene's obsession with the subject of divided loyalties, a subject dramatically fixed in his mind while at Berkhamsted School, where he had to deal with conflicting loyalties to his father, the school, and his peers. Greene later found a way of escaping the conflict and puts his solution forward through the character of Javitt, in "Under the Garden": "If you have to earn a living, boy, and the price they make you pay is loyalty, be a double-agent—and never let either of the two sides know your real name" (*CS*, 216). David is Greene's first attempt to create such a character, but it would be many more years before Greene could flesh him out with complex and believable motivation.

The comic phase of Greene's career is represented in *The Last Word* by two stories that appeared in *Punch*, "Work Not in Progress" (1955) and "The Man Who Stole the Eiffel Tower" (1956). It was about this time that Greene was writing *Our Man in Havana*, a novel that captures a comic view of life that Greene, in his depressive mood, denied his previous heroes. His cocky state of well-being at the time is brilliantly embodied in the character of that novel's hero, James Wormold, a fellow with the unique sanity of the clown. Unfortunately, Greene's two pieces in *Punch* seem hollow when compared to that novel.

Conceived as a sketch for a musical comedy, "Work Not in Progress" offers this bizarre plot: a group of 12 Anglican bishops are kidnapped by 12 thugs who hope to steal their chasubles belonging to the Church of England. The thugs are so poorly educated they have mistaken the word "chasuble" for "chalice." After a successful kidnapping, the thugs put on the bishops' clothes. The ringleader and brains of the gang is a woman (the only woman in the cast), and she assumes the role of Archbishop of Canterbury. Meanwhile, the Archbishop of Melbourne, who has come to observe the convocation of bishops, attempts to track down the kidnappers. He locates them in Canterbury where, in the rose garden, he falls in love with the false Archbishop of Canterbury. Later the rest of the gang realize they have been betrayed by their leader and attack her. She is defended by the Bishop of Melbourne until the arrival of the true bishops in their underclothes scares away the impostors. The musical ends with the lovers singing a melodious duet and then heading off to live together in Australia.

Hardly up to the standards of W. S. Gilbert, this fantasy sketch of a musical comedy may have titillated some readers of *Punch* at the time but the piece does not hold up very well. It seems more suited now to undergraduate tastes that have come to savor the Monty Python brand of comedy. The slapstick humor of presenting 12 bishops running across the stage in their underwear and of having a female thug dress up like the Archbishop of Canterbury shows Greene shamelessly indulging in the pleasures of low comedy.

"The Man Who Stole the Eiffel Tower" opens with a riveting sentence and then lapses into disappointing frivolity: "It was not so much the theft of the Eiffel Tower which caused me difficulty; it was putting it back before anyone noticed" (*Last Word*, 44). The narrator describes how he hired a fleet of trucks to carry the Eiffel Tower out of Paris to a quiet, flat field on the way to Chantilly. Having great affection for the structure, he is pleased to see it "after all those years of war and fog and rain and radar, in repose" (*Last Word*, 41). Greene's anti-Americanism then surfaces as he has the narrator return to the empty site to enjoy the confusion of stupid American tourists. Finally, the narrator returns the Eiffel Tower before the employees who work there lose their wages.

The comic stories are the weakest in the collection. They are not especially funny, their humor is undergraduate and patronizing, they feature no notable characters, and their whimsy and fantasy are contrived. Perhaps Greene had poured all of his comic genius into writing the novel *Our Man in Havana* (1958). In any event, one suspects he included the comic pieces in *The Last Word* to reflect what he calls his manic mood, the dynamic state of mind that gave birth to such brilliant comic characters as James Wormold (*Our Man in Havana*) and Aunt Augusta (*Travels with My Aunt*).

"An Appointment with the General" was originally published in 1982 under the title "On the Way Back: A Work Not in Progress" in *Firebird 1*, as part of a collection of fiction by contemporary authors. Greene's subtitle refers to the fact that this story is actually a chapter of an abortive novel that was to have been called *On the Way Back*. He conceived the idea of writing the novel in 1976, when he was invited to visit Panama as the guest of General Omar Torrijos Herrera. The invitation led to a curious friendship between the two men that lasted until the general's mysterious death in a plane crash in 1981. Greene eventually abandoned his novel *On the Way Back* in favor of writing a memoir of his friendship with Torrijos entitled *Getting to Know the General* (1984).

While being shown around Panama by the general's companion, a man named Chuchu, Greene picked up the title for his novel: "I heard Chuchu tell Captain Wong that we should see him again 'on the way back' "—Captain Wong, the miraculous Christ, the Haunted House, all were promised on the way back and my projected novel with that title again emerged from the shadows. In my book the promised return would never be fulfilled—there would be no going back for my chief character."[23] Later Greene entered a note in his diary for the new novel: "Start novel with a girl from a French left-wing weekly interviewing the General. She's escaping the pain of an unsatisfactory marriage in Paris and wants to avoid further pain. In the end she goes back to her pain and not to happiness" (*General*, 57).

Greene's note provides the outline for the surviving chapter "An Appointment with the General," but in *Getting to Know the General* he tells Chuchu the plot of the rest of the novel. He believes that in telling the story to his companion he had no further need to write it: "it is a substitute for the writing" (*General*, 57). Greene's idea was to have the general assign Chuchu to show the French journalist around Panama. She and Chuchu fall in love but he is later killed by a bomb someone planted in his car. The general has the journalist flown back to Panama City by helicopter and she must see from the air all the places Chuchu promised they would enjoy on the way back.

"An Appointment with the General" opens with the French journalist, Marie-Claire Duval, awaiting her interview with Torrijos. She feels dislocated, not knowing the language and feeling threatened by the men, dressed in camouflaged uniforms and carrying revolvers, who stand around her. One of the men, Sergeant Guardián (drawn after Chuchu), announces in perfect English that the general will see her but she cannot bring her tape recorder into the interview. She thinks, "I'll have to trust to my memory, my damnable memory, the memory I hate" (*Last Word*, 140).

The story then flashes back in time a month to the lunch she has with the editor of a left-wing French newspaper. Eager to discredit Torrijos, the editor praises Marie-Clair for her destructive interview with Helmut Schmidt and assigns her to interview the general. During the course of their conversation Greene makes it clear that the journalist will be no match for the general. She only knows French and English, knows little of geography, is dependent upon her tape recorder, and is psychologically flawed by a failing marriage. She accepts the assignment, in fact, to escape the memory of her loveless marriage.

The last section of the story focuses upon the interview, during which Guardián serves as the translator. Greene portrays the general as a wise, almost mystical figure, whose eyes are "laden with the future" (*Last Word*, 146). In his quiet way, he undermines the destructive agenda of Marie-Claire. Her attempts to label him a Marxist or socialist are met with clever parables: "My General says the Communists are for a while traveling on the same train as he is. So are the socialists. But it is he who is driving the train. It is he who will decide at what station to stop, and not his passengers" (*Last Word*, 149). Out of her own failed sexuality she desperately conjures up questions that would link the general's political power with sexual promiscuity: "What does he dream of? At night I mean. Does he dream of women. . . . Or does he dream of the terms he is going to make with the gringos?" (*Last Word*, 149). "The tired and wounded eyes looked at the wall behind her," Greene writes. "She could even understand the single phrase he spoke in reply to her question. '*El Muerte*.' 'He dreams of death,' the sergeant translated unnecessarily, and I could build an article on that, she thought with self-hatred" (*Last Word*, 149–50).

This story reflects Greene's own failed marriage and his hero-worshipping friendship with Torrijos. Like Marie-Claire, Greene enjoyed an exciting escape from domestic concerns upon receiving an invitation to meet with the general. It must have been an exhilarating experience for him to be taken into this leader's confidence, to be shown secret military plans, and be taken into the inner sanctum of political revolution. The character of Marie-Claire, however, not only embodies some of Greene's initial trepidations at meeting the general but serves to typify what Greene assumes are the Left's mistaken preconceived notions about Torrijos. Her vulnerability and weakness in the face of a third world savior mark her as one who, had the novel been completed, would have discovered the powerful inner resources of Greene's political hero. Ending as it does, however, the story merely sets up a straw-woman whose own decaying marriage leads her to self-hatred.

In "The Moment of Truth," originally published in the *Independent*

Part 1

Magazine on 18, June 1988, the 83-year-old Greene turns his thoughts to the subject of death. He opens his story with a characteristically surprising simile: "The near approach of death is like a crime which one is ashamed to confess to friends or fellow workers, and yet there remains a longing to confide in someone—perhaps a stranger in the street" (*Last Word*, 32). The hero of this story is Arthur Burton, a waiter in a London restaurant, who develops a fondness for an American couple, the Hogminsters, who, in appreciation of his solicitude, habitually sit at one of his tables.

A lonely man, Arthur lives in a small bed-sitting-room, and in the evenings enjoys a vicarious life by thinking of his various customers: dull married couples, young lovers interested only in each other, and, sometimes, married young women accompanied by older men. Arthur's sense of isolation is painfully exacerbated by his doctor's recent suspicion that he may have cancer: "the crime of death had touched him" (*Last Word*, 33). Like a criminal, he becomes desperate to confide his illness in someone. Touched by the use of his first name and the smile of real friendship that he received from Mrs. Hogminster, he decides to make her his confidante before he returns to his doctor for the final results of his medical tests.

The next day he discloses only a small portion of his secret to her when he announces he will not be at the restaurant tomorrow because he has to go to the hospital for a checkup. The Hogminsters offer him some platitudes of reassurance and tell him they will return for another meal before they leave for America. On his day off, they add, they plan to take his earlier advice and shop at some men's stores in Jermyn Street. That night he has a dream about Mrs. Hogminster: "It was as though he had spoken to her and somehow she had given him words of sympathy which lent him courage to face his enemies, who were about to disclose the shameful truth" (*Last Word*, 36).

The doctors inform Arthur that he does, indeed, have cancer and must be operated upon immediately. Although he is not frightened at the prospect of death, he wants "to share his knowledge and his secret with a stranger who would not be seriously affected like a wife or a child—he possessed neither—but might with a word of kindly interest share with him this criminal secret" (*Last Word*, 37–38). Convinced Mrs. Hogminster is just such a woman ("he had read it in her eyes"), Arthur arranges to return to work in the hope of talking to her.

To his dismay, he discovers the manager has seated the Hogminsters at another table. When he goes over to speak with them he is disappointed at their failure to inquire about his health. All they talk about are the details of their shopping spree in Jermyn Street. Arthur excuses himself and goes into the kitchen in a state of depression: "He was going to say nothing to the manager: the next day he would simply not turn up. The hospital could inform them in due course if he were dead or alive" (*Last Word*, 39).

Some moments later, however, the manager enters the kitchen and hands Arthur a letter from Mrs. Hogminster. Feeling immense relief, he reasons she could not discuss his secret in the restaurant for others to hear and therefore discreetly placed her inquiry and sympathy within this letter. He returns to the hospital for his operation and that night, before putting out the light over his bed, he opens and reads the letter. Mrs. Hogminster wrote: "Dear Arthur, I felt I must write you a word of thanks before we catch our plane. We have so enjoyed our visits to Chez Augustine and shall certainly return one day. And the Sales, we got such wonderful bargains—you were so right about Jermyn Street" (*Last Word*, 40).

The droll humor of this story is reminiscent of Greene's tales in *May We Borrow Your Husband?*. And, as in the latter volume, the comic pathos is worked out within the confines of a restaurant, an establishment that Greene employs as a workshop for his imagination. The technique of a doctor giving a death sentence to his patient was employed much earlier in "Under the Garden" where, stirred by his diagnosis, Wilditch seeks wholeness by returning to his childhood. Now the older Greene depicts his hero's impending death as a crime, something too shameful to be told to one's family or friends, as if death were a conscious betrayal of one's communal bond, a betrayal that would inflict pain and elicit hopeless sympathy. The irony of Mrs. Hogminster's letter, however, amplifies the folly of Arthur's attempt to secure sympathy and encouragement from outside the circle of his family or friends. Greene makes it clear in his story that Arthur was in the habit of observing his customers superficially. Like the hack writer in "The Invisible Japanese Gentlemen," Arthur fails to see what is really going on around him. Unlike the self-deluded writer, however, Arthur's failure to read the truth in Mrs. Hogminster's eyes leads to his utter disillusionment and desolation at the end of the story. The panic fear inherent in the human condition, from which Greene finds release through his writing, blossoms like a cancer in the moment of truth and disillusionment effected not by the doctor's diagnosis but by Mrs. Hogminster's letter.

"The Last Word," published in the *Independent Magazine* on 10 September, 1988, moves the subject of death beyond the dreary, localized confines of the preceding story to a futuristic brave new world where great spiritual heroism offers the hope of life after death. The last surviving Christian, an old man who turns out to be the last pope, has been living in a state of amnesia for the past 20 years, ever since he was shot during an assassination attempt. He is brought out of his humble apartment to meet the general of the new godless world union. He gradually recalls fragments from the past that reveal to him that he is indeed the pope, and he discovers that the general now plans to execute him.

As in *The Power and the Glory*, *The Comedians*, and *Monsignor Quixote*, Greene reverts to one of his favorite themes: the dramatic struggle between secular and spiritual power. Vaguely recalling Huxley's and Orwell's secular utopias, Greene's futuristic world boasts of peace through the elimination of poverty, nationalism, and Christianity. The general preserved the old man until he was sure that all of his followers were dead. On this occasion of their historical meeting, the general has the old man dressed in his formal papal robes, the clothes having been borrowed from the Museum of Myths. Over the years the old man has kept his Bible and a crucifix with one of Christ's arms broken off.

When the general tells the old man he feels sorry for his having lived so long in such dreary conditions, the man replies "They were not so dreary as you think. I had a friend with me. I could talk to him" (*Last Word*, 17). The general, failing to understand the reference is to the broken Christ on his cross, protests that his men assured him the old man was living alone all those years. Upon learning that he will now be executed, the old man expresses his relief: "You will be sending me where I've often wanted to go during the last twenty years." "Into darkness?" asks the general. "Oh, the darkness I have known was not death," says the old man. "You are sending me into the light. I am grateful to you" (*Last Word*, 18).

As a symbol of final friendship between two born to be enemies, the general pours out two glasses of wine, a moment that suggests the Last Supper of Christ. The old man raises his glass as though in salute and says in a low voice some words in a language that the general cannot understand: "Corpus domini nostri. . . ." These are the words of the priest during the Communion service of the Mass. As the old man drinks his wine the general shoots and kills him. In this reenactment of the Last Supper, the old man presumably reverts to his former priestly duties and consecrates the wine as the blood of Christ. By shooting the old man (the pope, Christ's representative on earth), the general reenacts the combined roles of Judas and Pontius Pilate.

Greene adds a final paragraph to his story, however, that undermines the secular convictions of the general: "Between the pressure on the trigger and the bullet exploding a strange and frightening doubt crossed his mind: is it possible that what this man believed may be true?" (*Last Word*, 18). This suggestion of a lingering doubt in the general's vision of a godless world seems totally unprepared for by the rest of the story. Greene seems to be reaching back a few years to *Monsignor Quixote* for his conclusion here. In that novel the representative of the Marxist state, the mayor, attends a final Mass said in pantomime by the dying Monsignor Quixote. Having no chalice or Host, Monsignor Quixote nevertheless places an imaginary wafer upon the mayor's tongue. The mayor, feeling the pressure, wonders later if he might not in fact have received Communion. Greene deftly leaves the Marxist mayor with a troubling ambiguity that suggests his capability for belief in God. The amicable relationship between the mayor and Quixote, however, is established throughout the novel, making its conclusion credible. The relationship between the general and the pope in "The Last Word," on the other hand, is abstract and undeveloped, and the conclusion seems forced.

Greene would have done better to have followed the more rigid pattern of *The Power and the Glory*. Like the general of "The Last Word," the lieutenant in *The Power and the Glory* has spent his life eradicating Christianity from his country. Also like the general, he is dedicated to eliminating the poverty and suffering of his people. What makes him so effective in his work is his total, unflagging belief in the rightness of his socialist program. Having brought about the capture and execution of the whisky priest, the lieutenant may miss his quarry but he entertains no misgivings about his faith in the secular state. Greene's general thus comes across as someone with an even grander accomplishment than that of the lieutenant—a worldwide socialist state—and on whose character Greene grafts the susceptibility of the genial Communist mayor from *Monsignor Quixote*. The hybrid character is not convincing.

"An Old Man's Memory" originally appeared in the *Independent Magazine* on 25 November, 1989. Although designated "a new short story by Graham Greene," the piece, less than a thousand words long, reads more like a dire warning to the English government about the potential for sabotage of the Channel Tunnel between Dover and Calais, scheduled for completion in 1994. The narrator of Greene's story, writing in the year 1995, announces that the year 1994 will never cease to horrify him: "The event of that year has a quality of nightmare about it—deaths in the darkness, in the depths of the sea, deaths by mutilation and drowning. The rotting bodies of the unrecognizable lie even today on both sides of the Channel" (*Last Word*, 77).

The narrator (clearly no prophet) recalls Margaret Thatcher, having won her fourth electoral contest, greeting the French train as it comes up from the sea and halts at Dover to join the celebration. On the other side of the Channel the president of France awaits the British train, but it never arrives. Bombs have exploded under the Channel and the British train is destroyed along with the lives of all the people aboard it. Two years have passed since the disaster and the terrorists have not been identified or captured.

Greene borrows several details from recent terrorist activities to build his case for the dangers involved in the tunnel. Semtex appears to have been the explosive used in the tunnel and the narrator reminds us that in the late 1980s only 300 grams of Semtex were needed to blow up the Pan American plane over Lockerbie, Scotland. Now, he argues, explosives can be timed days, not hours, in advance.

The prime suspect, of course, is the IRA, but he also points to the Iranians, who had never forgiven England for its support of Salman Rushdie nor the Americans for having shot down their innocent airliner. There were, he observes, more Americans on board the train than there were English.

After noting the British and French governments' plan to reopen the tunnel by 1997, he concludes his account by predicting the public's reluctance to reenter the tunnel. Quite clearly Greene is here putting his fiction into the service of propaganda. Over the years Greene wrote hundreds of letters to newspapers and magazines in which he protested or criticized the actions of many governments and institutions. "An Old Man's Memory" is simply a more interesting form in which to cast his argument than the conventional letter to the editor. Several people in England had already pointed out the possibility that the IRA could blow up the tunnel. Greene's idea is not new, but the weight of his reputation as a novelist and his futuristic point of view perhaps give the story more political clout than a nameless activist could achieve in a television interview. But he does weaken the credibility of his narrator by having Margaret Thatcher still prime minister in 1995. The view of Westminster from Antibes had apparently grown somewhat hazy.

Published for the first time, "A Branch of the Service" is a comic account of an employee of a restaurant-rating association who is recruited by the Secret Service to eavesdrop on suspicious diners. Now retired, the narrator announces that he reluctantly left his profession because he lost his appetite for food.

Reminiscent of the professional eavesdroppers (and Greene himself) in the restaurants of Antibes (*May We Borrow Your Husband?*), the narrator observes his fellow diners with the analytical eye and ear of a writer. In one case his astute observation leads him to retrieve a cigarette containing some secret information of interest to the government. The cigarette leads to a new suspect, a doctor who had connections with the chemical industry, and the narrator is assigned to watch him. During the lengthy meal, however, the narrator is struck by diarrhea and after he returns from the toilet the doctor has vanished. Embarrassed by his failure, the narrator decides to retire.

Bathroom humor has a long tradition in England and Greene seems to delight in it. Years earlier in *Our Man in Havana* he drew a very funny scene in which the hero, James Wormold, is recruited into the Secret Service in a public toilet. Javitt, in "Under the Garden," sits upon a filthy commode, and Beauty, the pampered Pekinese in "Beauty," rolls in a clump of offal during an unscheduled spree.

Misbegotten Tales

Greene's decision to exclude from *Collected Stories* and *The Last Word* the tales he wrote during his student days at Berkhamsted School and Oxford is understandable. In those early pieces, written between 1920 and 1925, he was coming to terms with questions of religious belief, personal betrayal, and romantic idealism. He was experimenting with serious fiction for the first time in his life and laying the groundwork for the novels he was to publish during the next decade.

Some of the stories Greene wrote during his mature years, however, have also been excluded from *Collected Stories* and *The Last Word*. These include *The Bear Fell Free* (published in book form in 1935), "The Other Side of the Border" (a novel fragment dated 1936 and included in *Nineteen Stories*), "Voyage in the Dark" (1938), "The Escapist" (1939), and "All But Empty" (1947). Greene apparently feels that these stories do not represent his best work in the genre; furthermore, he makes no acknowledgment of them in his various writings. These misbegotten tales, nevertheless, are interesting for the light they shed upon Greene's style, themes, and psychology.

Shortly after his return in 1935 from his dangerous and rugged exploration of Liberia, Greene experienced a burst of creative activity, correcting the proofs of his novel *England Made Me*, beginning another novel, *A Gun for Sale*, completing "The Basement Room," and writing two other short stories, "Jubilee" and *The Bear Fell Free*.

The Bear Fell Free was published in book form by Grayson and Grayson in 1935. The publisher himself selected 12 authors and published a short story by each author as a separate book. Choosing writers he believed would later become famous, Grayson proved himself prophetic in many of his selections, which also included H. E. Bates, Arthur Calder-Marshall, and Sean O'Faoláin.

The hero of Greene's story is Tony Farrell, an irresponsible and reckless character, drawn possibly after Greene's eldest brother, Herbert. Having won some money in the Irish Sweepstakes, Tony celebrates his good fortune by throwing a party. After drinking five glasses of sherry, he accepts a challenge to fly across the Atlantic. Before he sets off, his girlfriend, Jane, throws a teddy bear in the back seat of his small plane. Tony runs into bad weather, crashes the plane, and is killed, but the stuffed bear falls free.

Carter, Tony's friend, retrieves the bear and returns it to Jane, who is sleeping with another man. Frivolous and selfish, she not only betrays Tony while she believed him alive and flying across the Atlantic, but later sleeps with Carter, filling him with a sense of guilt. The name Carter, of course, recalls the boy of the same name who betrayed Greene's romantic innocence at Berkhamsted School.

The style of *The Bear Fell Free* is unique among all of Greene's short stories. Through the technique of a third-person stream of consciousness Greene attempts to reflect the workings of Tony's mind as he flies across the ocean to his death as well as the drifting thoughts of several other characters. The narrative, comprised of dialogue and clipped and fragmented phrases and sentences, moves freely between the past and the present, from the cockpit to the party, and from the plane crash to Jane's bedroom.

The story's final paragraph best illustrates Greene's experimental style. It comes right after the description of Tony Farrell's crash into the water at a 120 miles an hour. His neck is broken and his knees are struck upward, in a fetal position, the broken bones jabbing through the broken neck. The character named Baron, mentioned below, is a friend of Tony's, a socialist dreamer who dies of a heart attack in his bathtub. The passage reads:

> Birth and death simultaneously tainted with each other. Guilt and suicide in the maternity ward, guilt and suicide in the trenches, in Jane's flat guilt and suicide. Patient serious Baron, tasting from the first of the final soapsud, soapsuds in settlements, soapsuds in Parliament, soapsuds in Buckingham Palace. Money for nothing wrenched from Mrs. Farrell's womb, sherry circulating through the broken neck, unbearable agony of the cracked skull in Jane's bed. Prayers no good for something already happened, memory of good with no past, hope no good with no future, love no good with no end and no beginning.
> The teddy bear fell free.[24]

There are thematic and stylistic connections between this story and *England Made Me*, the novel that Greene completed shortly before writing *The Bear Fell Free*. Although employing a conventional third-person narrative in *England Made Me*, Greene occasionally presents the thoughts of his hero, Anthony Farrant, by means of an interior monologue. Furthermore, the heroes of both stories have similar names: Anthony Farrant and Tony Farrell. Both characters are hollow men fated for failure. Their interest lies in their cleverness, their tireless energy and false dreams, and in the emotional wreckage they leave behind them.

Although "The Other Side of the Border" is a fragment of a novel Greene abandoned writing after his return from Liberia in 1935, he decided to include it as one of the tales in *Nineteen Stories* (1947). He writes that he discovered the manuscript and as he read it "the characters, the scene and the half-unfolded story seemed to me to have more interest than many tales of mine that had appeared fully dressed between covers. Why shouldn't this book, too, I felt, have its chance?[25] He gives two reasons why he abandoned the novel: first, he was busy writing a more compelling book, *Brighton Rock*; and second, he had already dealt with the main character in a novel called *England Made Me* (1935). "Hands, I realized," he writes, "had the same origin as Anthony Farrent [sic] in that novel" (*Nineteen Stories*, 211).

Greene's personal attachment to both *England Made Me* and "The Other Side of the Border" derives from the fact that he based the characters of both Anthony Farrant and Hands on his eldest brother, Herbert, the black sheep of the family. Herbert was a calculating, irresponsible, alcoholic adventurer. He took various jobs in far-off places such as Rhodesia and Brazil but was always in debt and fated for failure. He demanded an audience for extravagant and dishonest stories about his adventures as if, thereby, he could validate his fantasies and justify his failures. Greene probably took the name Hands for his character from a teacher at Berkhamsted School who was fired by his father. Like Herbert, Hands was a loser (Sherry 1989–, 1:502).

The story begins in the present as a young man named Morrow, recently returned from his duties in West Africa, reports to his employer, Mr. Danvers, the manager of a gold-mining syndicate. Sick with yellow fever, Morrow attempts to warn Mr. Danvers about Hands, the man he hired to lead the expedition two years earlier. Morrow resigns from the company and insists on revealing the horrifying events that took place under Hands: "The whole business—it's fantastic. The gold—and Hands himself—so many deaths—Colley—and then there's Billings." When Mr. Danvers says that he has absolute trust in Hands's judgment, Morrow replies, "That's why I've resigned. You mustn't trust it too far. You've got to know—the Board have got to know—"

(*Nineteen Stories*, 214) but the violent onset of chills keeps him from completing his sentence.

This opening section of the story draws heavily upon Conrad's *The Heart of Darkness*. Morrow's stifled report suggests that Hands, like Mr. Kurtz, once on his own, away from the constraints of civilization, has degenerated into a brutal savage. It is later stated that Morrow calculates that hundred of blacks died while working under Hands. And in Morrow's dialogue, quoted above, there is the sinister implication that Colley and Billings, two fellow Britishers working under Hands, are also dead.

The story then shifts back in time and focuses upon Hands, out of work, broke, and restless in his hometown village of Denton (carefully drawn after Greene's own town of Berkhamsted). The relationship between Hands and his father parallels that between Herbert Greene and his father. Mr. Hands "was a Liberal, he thought men could govern themselves if they were left alone to it, that wealth did not corrupt and that statesmen loved their country" (*Nineteen Stories*, 217). His image of the world, however, is breaking up now that his wife has died and Hands has proven himself to be a failure, a person who comes home regularly "with his excuses and breezy anecdotes and unjustified contempt" (*Nineteen Stories*, 217). Hands lectures his father, "It's no good being a Liberal in these times. . . . You don't realize here in Denton. I've been about the world . . ." (*Nineteen Stories*, 218).

Hands finally grows restless and, falsifying his previous work experiences, applies for work overseas. When he receives an encouraging letter from Mr. Danvers, he travels to Liverpool, interviews for the job, and, to his amazement, is hired to lead an expedition into a West African port in search of gold. It is as if Greene is here transferring his own youthful fantasies, inspired by *King Solomon's Mines*, to his childish and irresponsible hero. Having written "The Other Side of the Border" shortly after returning from his own expedition into Liberia, Greene could well imagine the moral destruction of his eldest brother under similar circumstances.

Mr. Danvers, concerned about the public relations of his syndicate, engages a reporter to depict Hands as a man of extraordinary character, an adventurer like Sir Walter Raleigh. His description of Hands again recalls that of Mr. Kurtz: "These niggers need to be impressed. In a way, you know, the man who leads this expedition is an ambassador—the ambassador of Europe, of civilization" (*Nineteen Stories*, 234). Mr. Danvers, of course, is as corrupt as Hands. His chief concern is to exploit the hidden wealth of an uncivilized country on "the other side of the border."

The second section of the story, set in West Africa, establishes the same sort of seedy atmosphere that Greene later used in his descriptions of Mexico. The dominant images are those of blazing heat and birds of prey that "squatted like domestic pigeons on the roofs, turning their little moron heads this way and that, spying for carrion" (*Nineteen Stories*, 238).

Hands, Billings, Colley, and Morrow, all failures, are thrown together in this demoralizing atmosphere. Hands, however, is able to inspire his fellow adventurers by feeding their fantasies of grand achievements and the promise of wealth. Billings reflects upon the chance for a new life: "A whole crowd who've never had a proper chance. Sneered at. Sacked. And then suddenly—the day comes, and it's we—" (*Nineteen Stories*, 245). Hands, Billings, and Colley despise young Morrow for his priggishness, for his sense of moral superiority. The story ends with Colley's condemnation of Morrow and his celebration of friendship with Hands and Billings: "we are all alike."

As the opening of the story reveals, only Morrow manages to redeem himself by returning to England and attempting to report the horrors his former comrades appear to have worked upon the natives during their unchronicled expedition of two years. The story, of course, is unfinished. Greene writes that "I remember the characters in the book well—Hands, young Morrow, Billings—I can't remember what was going to happen to them" (*Nineteen Stories*, 210–11).

A major problem with "The Other Side of the Border" is that there are too many failed characters competing for attention. The theme of failure is central to many of Greene's later works, but he usually manages to keep the theme focused upon a single character. He handles the scenes with Hands and his father especially well, but the several pages given over to descriptions of Colley's train trip and his reflections upon his past failures in Brazil and Africa put this character in a discomforting competition with the hero, Hands. Later, when Greene introduces Billings and his failed mission in the church, the focus of the story is further distorted. It is not clear how Greene could have developed an interesting relationship among these three characters. Perhaps he had in mind not only *The Heart of Darkness* but Kipling's "The Man Who Would Be King," in which two British scoundrels manage to outwit a remote tribe of natives and establish themselves as their supreme rulers.

Greene's travels through Mexico in 1938 proved to be one of the most stimulating and creative periods of his life. Within less than two years he wrote *The Lawless Roads*, *The Power and the Glory*, and several short stories, all based upon his experiences in Mexico. Here was a land that was configured for his imagination: Catholic, violent, alien, and very exciting. While *The Lawless Roads* and *The Power and the Glory* embody Greene's obsessions on a broad scale, his uncollected Mexican story "Voyage in the Dark" (1938) reveals his compulsive search for danger and his unabashed delight in shabby and seedy surroundings.

Like Greene, the unnamed narrator of "Voyage in the Dark" is an Englishman roughing it in Mexico. Looking for a boat that will take him from Vera Cruz to Tabasco, he is warned by the local consul that he is a fool, that no foreigner has ever traveled on one of the small boats because they are too dangerous. The narrator then takes up with a guide, a dapper young man, and after they share several drinks together, the young man insists upon taking the boat with him in order to prove a Mexican is as good a sport as an Englishman.

Greene's description of the run-down boat is rendered in loving detail as if to inform his comfortable middle-class English readers (the story appeared in the *Spectator*)that real life is not to be found aboard a Cunard liner:

> We came to it in a taxi with my single suitcase, bumping over the Vera Cruz quay. An English pleasure liner of about ten thousand tons, a few coaling steamers, out in the gulf a grey gunboat. "There's the 'Ruiz Cano,'" the taximan said. I couldn't see it anywhere: I looked right over the top of the ship where it lay against the quay—a barge of about a hundred tons with a few feet of broken rail, an old funnel you could almost touch with your hand, a bell hanging on a torn piece of string, an oil lamp, and a bundle of turkeys. One little rotting lifeboat dangled inadequately from the davits.[26]

The Mexican guide meets his nine-year-old nephew and boasts to him that he is taking the boat to prove what a good sport he is and then turns to the people gathered at the quay and makes the boast again, winning the admiration of the strangers. No sooner than he is on board, however, he decides that his nephew needs him, and he makes a frantic jump back onto the shore.

In the final paragraph of the story Greene renders the theme of the dangerous voyage, the deliberate move into the unknown and the irrational, through the imagery of light and darkness: "There was no light at all on the little deck and none below: only the oil lamp in the bows. The searchlights of the English liner moved right over our heads, missing us altogether, and the captain began to enter his log by the light of an electric torch a sailor held for him. After an hour one bare globe went on outside the sleeping cells, above a tin washbasin, and the wind rose. We chugged in almost complete darkness out into the Gulf" ("Voyage," 437).

While Greene skillfully captures the atmosphere of the run-down port and conveys the thrill of setting out into the unknown, the texture of the story is rather thin. One of the major problems with "Voyage in the Dark" is Greene's failure to develop the character of his narrator, which makes his account read like a piece of impressionistic journalism.

Greene published a second story in the *Spectator* the following year. "The Escapist" (1939), probably written about the same time as "Voyage in the Dark" and arising out of Greene's travels through Mexico, focuses upon the theme of escape. Whereas "Voyage in the Dark" focuses upon the narrator's escape from the safe constraints of English civilization as he recklessly rides the Atlantic in the Gulf of Mexico for 42 hours, "The Escapist" centers upon the dangerous exploits of a German criminal named K., a restless man who has traveled around the world seeking freedom and peace, whose ambition is to escape to an idyllic world of isolation on the Amazon.

The unnamed narrator, traveling on a ship from Vera Cruz, meets K. as he is brought aboard between two detectives. The story consists of piecing together the story of this mysterious figure, a true Greene hero, a rebel against social orthodoxy, a refugee from civilization seeking peace in the jungles of South America. Although Greene used the name K. for one of his villains in a novel he was writing at the time, *The Confidential Agent*, K. is really the prototype of Querry, the civilization-sick hero of *A Burnt-Out Case* who looks for peace in a remote African leprosarium.

Arrested in Tapechula for not having travel papers, K. was imprisoned in a wretched jail ("the floor crawled with worms") for three months where he shared his time with drunks and murderers. The narrator observes that K. "was what we call now an escapist. It came out in scraps, during the fortnight's voyage in no chronological order, like a Conrad novel, but when you put them together the scraps fitted. An extraordinary sense of goodness surrounded him."[27]

The narrator records the various stages of K.'s escapes. In 1913, at age 19, K. left Germany because he feared there was going to be a war. In New York he worked as a fireman in an ice factory, then helped with rowing boats on the Hudson, but after his employer wanted him to marry, K. left that job and joined a circus. After the war he worked on an old British freighter until, in Liverpool, he was repatriated and sent back to Germany. After a run-in with a German ship captain, K. enlisted in the Foreign Legion for two years. He later went to live in Spain, but when a friend, a German painter with two wives, wanted K. to marry, K. took a shop to the Amazon, where he finally found his paradise among the Iquito Indians.

One of the driving themes in Greene's fiction, the relentless quest for peace, lies at the heart of this story. The narrator observes that K.'s random conversation would always come back to his ambition to be settled on the Amazon: "He had once spent six months there, far up over the Peruvian border, on a tributary . . . and he was going back. Nobody could stop him. When he spoke of it he was like a lover, and like a lover he brought the beloved name into every conversation. . . . and you knew he was away in a land where a man could live on nothing, without violence or hate. . . . —and there was nothing to worry about any more for ever" ("Escapist," 48).

The story of K. is, of course, the story of Greene himself, of his lifelong series of escapes from reality through travel and, more importantly, through his imaginative reconstruction of reality. Greene refers to his short stories as escapes from the arduous task of writing novels. In his significantly titled autobiography, *Ways of Escape*, he argues that the very act of writing is a way of escaping "the panic fear which is inherent in the human condition." In these escapes one faces a series of risks and moral choices as he pursues the idyllic dream. The dangers are betrayal, corruption, and failure.

Here, then, in 1939, in the character of K. can be found the elusive dream that motivates such later heroes as Scobie (*The Heart of the Matter*), Wilditch ("Under the Garden"), and Querry (*A Burnt-Out Case*). K.'s numerous literal escapes may now be over as he heads toward a prison in Germany, but he can always escape into the dream of his safe and peaceful home on the Amazon among the Iquitos.

Published in the *Strand Magazine* in 1947, "All But Empty" is an inferior version of "A Little Place off the Edgeware Road" (1939); I suspect that it was written before 1939.[28] In the magazine the story is "decorated by Brian Robb" with dark, shadowy drawings of the characters. These crude illustrations seem to parody rather than complement the intended sinister atmosphere of the story. The editor of the magazine further trivializes the piece with his commercial headnote: "No other writer can create suspense, or produce a shudder, quite like Graham Greene. Here, in a story you can read in five minutes, is some of the distilled essence of the master."[29]

The narrator of "All But Empty" explains his habit of attending a seedy cinema showing silent films. He goes there because "it was silent, because it was all but empty and because the girl who sold the tickets had a bright, common, venal prettiness" ("Empty," 66). He is alone in the theater one day when an elderly man sits beside him even though he had the whole cinema to choose from. He feels the old man's damp beard brush his face as he passes him to take his seat. The stranger begins sobbing and whispering that he can neither see nor hear the picture. Assuming that the old man is confused or blind, the narrator offers to show him to another cinema and then to take him home. The man refuses, saying that he always comes to this cinema. Then, brushing the narrator's lips with his damp beard, the pathetic old man announces: "No one could expect me to see, not after I've seen what I've seen. . . . From ear to ear" ("Empty," 67).

The old man goes on to describe a murder that took place earlier in the day. As he came down the stairs of his apartment in Seymour Terrace he saw on the landing a man smiling: "Oh, I was angry when he laughed: the knife trembled. And there the poor body lay with the throat cut from ear to ear" ("Empty," 69).

Fearing the man to be mad and dangerous, but believing his story, the narrator telephones the police to tell them that the murderer in the Seymour Terrace case is here with him in the theater. The police reply, "We've got the murderer. It's the body that's disappeared" ("Empty," 69).

Although this story shares the same plot with "A Little Place off the Edgeware Road," it never rises above slick melodrama. Neither the narrator nor the murdered man is a developed character. Each seems to exist merely to move the plot along to its surprise ending (in less than five minutes!). In "A Little Place off the Edgeware Road," in contrast, Greene writes from the omniscient point of view and develops the character of Craven as someone deranged by his morbid sensibilities. Craven's nightmarish vision of a zombielike community of corrupted bodies living on after death prepares the reader for his ghoulish encounter with a murdered man. "All But Empty" lacks this important psychological dimension and reads like a simple horror story, calculated for a cheap thrill.

Conclusion

During a career of almost 70 years Graham Greene established a reputation as one of the most popular and respected novelists of the twentieth century. His achievement as a writer of short stories has been compromised by his success as a novelist. Furthermore, Greene's own comment that his short stories are mere by-products of a novelist's career contributed to the critical neglect of his short fiction. Nevertheless, the Thames television production of "Shades of Greene" in 1976 (along with the paperback publication of his stories under the same title) and the publication of *The Last Word* in 1990 have helped to focus attention upon him as a writer of short fiction.

In the introduction to his *Collected Stories* Greene writes that "I have never written anything better than 'The Destructors,' 'A Chance for Mr. Lever,' 'Under the Garden,' 'Cheap in August,'" but he then goes on to qualify his achievement by noting that "I remain in this field a novelist who has happened to write short stories" (viii). One would be wise to take his second comment, which sounds suspiciously self-defensive, with a grain of salt. The four stories Greene names are clearly among his best writings, but to that list I would add "Across the Bridge," "The Basement Room," "I Spy," and "May We Borrow Your Husband?" Those stories best reveal Greene's genius for probing human psychology, creating atmospheres that illuminate and help to shape his vivid characters, and working out the mythic themes of lost innocence, betrayal, and rebirth.

Greene's short fiction is driven by his personal demons: a sense of betrayed innocence; an authoritarian and puritanical father; clever school bullies; fear of the dark, birds, and water; fear of and fascination with sexuality; and fear of boredom. As this study has attempted to demonstrate, Greene's short fiction serves as a means of exorcising or restraining these demons. The entire fabric of his fiction, from his earliest stories in the *Berkhamstedian* to *The Last Word*, reveals a continuous psychological thread. His incredibly prolific body of work—indeed, his very writing habits, such as his setting a goal to write a certain number of words each day and his careful tallying of his daily output—suggests a powerful compulsion to unburden himself of recurrent fears and anxieties and to fill up the hours of an otherwise threateningly empty day.

In overcoming his personal fear of boredom by writing and by traveling to exciting and sometimes dangerous places around the world, Greene ensured that his stories reflect his dynamic psychological drama and therefore offer the reader an equal opportunity to escape from boredom. While the quality of his stories is uneven, few of them, with perhaps the exception of some of his juvenilia, are ever boring. Greene is a skilled storyteller, an old-fashioned one in the best sense of the phrase.

Influenced by such writers as Henry James, Maupassant, V. S. Pritchett, and Somerset Maugham, Greene composed his stories along traditional lines, emphasizing character, atmosphere, and irony. The hallmark of his short fiction, as with his novels, can be found in his dramatic opening sentences, crisp dialogue, clever similes, seedy atmospheres, and recurrent themes such as lost innocence and betrayal. Although he tried his hand at an experimental style of writing in *The Bear Fell Free* and in some early novels, he quickly abandoned the stream-of-consciousness technique in favor of the more conventional third-person and occasional first-person narratives.

Greene's achievement as a short story writer lies in his ability to weave compelling tales that create a unique vision of the world. Thus fragments of conversations overheard in an Antibes restaurant or hotel are transformed into powerful dramas of lust, cruelty, love, and fear. Painful childhood memories are shown to shape one's entire adult life and to nourish an impossible desire to recapture a lost dream. When reviewed in their entirety, Greene's short stories reveal a lifelong psychodrama that reflects his addiction to excitement, travel, and writing itself. Further, these tales reveal his persistent battle with the demons of his youth and his ability to transform them into characters and themes and later to shape them into religious, political, and social issues. Thus the authoritarian father and the bullies of his youth become, in his later works, foreign dictators and their brutal henchmen, pious priests and laymen, and even ordinary adults (as in "The Basement Room") who contaminate the dreams of children.

Notes to Part 1

1. "Walter De La Mare's Short Stories," *Collected Essays* (London: Penguin, 1970), 108.

2. "The Tick of the Clock," *Berkhamstedian* 40 (December 1920): 119, hereafter cited in text as "Tick."

3. *A Sort of Life* (New York: Washington Square Press, 1973), 96–97; hereafter cited in text as *Sort*.

4. "The Poetry of Modern Life," *Berkhamstedian* 41 (March 1921): 3; hereafter cited in text as "Modern Life."

5. Norman Sherry, *The Life of Graham Greene*, (New York: Viking, 1989–), 1:81; hereafter cited in text.

6. "Castles in the Air," *Berkhamstedian* 41 (December 1921): 112; hereafter cited in text as "Castles."

7. Quoted in Sherry, *Life of Graham Greene*, 1:101. This is the only story I have been unable to locate. Sherry does not provide a reference for his quotation but his narrative implies that the story may have been published in 1921, perhaps in the *Weekly Westminster Gazette*. The British Library, however, has been unable to locate the piece for me in that periodical. Subsequent page references to this story are from Sherry and are indicated in the text.

8. Roland A. Wobbe, "Tyranny's Triangle: Patterns in Greene's Juvenilia and Major Works," *College Literature* 12 (1985): 4; hereafter cited in text.

9. "The Tyranny of Realism," *Berkhamstedian* 42 (March 1922): 3; hereafter cited in text as "Tyranny."

10. "Magic," *Weekly Westminster Gazette* 1 (6 May 1922): 16; hereafter cited in text as "Magic."

11. "The Trial of Pan," *Oxford Outlook* 5 (February 1923): 47; hereafter cited in text as "Pan."

12. "The Improbable Tale of the Archbishop of Canterbridge," *Cherwell*, n.s., 12 (15 November 1924): 187; hereafter cited in text as "Improbable Tale."

13. "The New House," *Oxford Outlook* 5 (November 1923): 114–15; hereafter cited in text as "New House."

14. "The Lord Knows," *Oxford Chronicle* 5 June 1925, p. 16; hereafter cited in text as "Lord Knows."

15. "The End of the Party," *Collected Stories* (London: Bodley Head/ William Heinemann, 1972), 557. Unless otherwise noted, all subsequent story quotations are from this edition, hereafter cited in text as *CS*.

16. See Richard Kelly, "Greene's Consuming Fiction," *College Literature* 12 (1985): 53–59.

17. Brian Thomas, *An Underground Fate: The Idiom of Romance in the Later Novels of Graham Greene* (Athens: University of Georgia Press, 1988), 103; hereafter cited in text.

18. Quoted in Marie-Françoise Allain, *The Other Man: Conversation with Graham Greene* (New York: Simon and Schuster, 1983), 162–63.

19. *Ways of Escape* (New York: Washington Square Press, 1982), 226; hereafter cited in text as *Ways*.

20. *Graphic*, 5 October 1929, p. 82.

21. *Graphic*, 19 October 1929, p. 132.

22. "Murder for the Wrong Reason," *The Last Word* (London: Reinhardt Books, 1990), 136. Unless otherwise noted, all subsequent quotations within this section are from this volume, hereafter cited as *Last Word*.

23. *Getting to Know the General* (London: Bodley Head, 1984), 54; hereafter cited in text as *General*.

24. *The Bear Fell Free* (London: Grayson and Grayson, 1935), 17–18.

25. "The Other Side of the Border," *Nineteen Stories* (New York: Viking, 1949), hereafter cited in text as *Nineteen Stories*.

26. "Voyage in the Dark," *Spectator* 161 (16 September 1938): 437; hereafter cited in text as "Voyage."

27. "The Escapist," *Spectator* 162 (13 January 1939): 48; hereafter cited in text as "Escapist."

28. When I asked Greene about this story he claimed to have no memory of its details or date of composition. Judging from such stylistic lapses as awkward syntax and repetition and the poorly developed melodramatic character of the story, I view this tale as a working draft of "A Little Place off the Edgeware Road."

29. "All But Empty," *Strand Magazine* 112 (March 1947): 66; hereafter cited in text as "Empty."

Part 2

THE WRITER

Introduction

Most of Graham Greene's comments about his writing may be found in his autobiographies, letters, prefaces, and in various interviews he granted over the years. Most of his observations, however, focus upon his novels and not upon his work in other genres. Despite the large number of short stories he has written, he has had little to say about them. Nevertheless, I have attempted to include in this part as much material as I could find that reveals his critical perspective on his short fiction.

His "Introduction" to the *Collected Stories* provides a valuable commentary upon the conception of these tales as well as some incisive insights into the psychological and creative forces that lie behind them. The selected passages from Greene's interview with Marie-Françoise Allain not only shed light on some of his specific stories but they provide an interesting critique of the role of the subconscious and dreams in his stories. Finally, the letters that Greene wrote to Elizabeth Bowen and V. S. Pritchett reveal his early and seminal thinking on such important topics as the writer's morality, his religious and social obligations, and his obligation to be "disloyal," views that he later transformed into the mythic texture of "Under the Garden."

Introduction to *Collected Stories*

I want to explain this collection rather than apologize for it, as I once did in a prefatory note to my first volume of *Nineteen Stories*. I thought then there would never be any further "scraps," as I think I called them. The short story as a form bothered me then and a little bored me. One knew too much about the story before one began writing—and then there were all the days of work unrelieved by any surprise. In the far longer work of the novel there were periods of great weariness, but at any moment the unexpected might happen—a minor character would suddenly take control and dictate his words and actions. Somewhere near the beginning, for no reason I knew, I would insert an incident which seemed entirely irrelevant, and sixty thousand words later, with a sense of excitement, I would realize why it was there—the narrative had been working all that time outside my conscious control. But in the short story I knew everything before I began to write—or so I thought.

I was reminded of the kind of essays we were taught to write at school—you were told to make first a diagram which showed the development of the argument, rather as later a film producer would sometimes talk to me of the necessity of "establishing" this or that and the imaginary value of "continuity." When school was safely behind me I began to write "essays" again. I learned to trust the divagations of the mind. If you let the reins loose the horse will find its way home. The shape was something which grew of itself *inside* the essay, during the revision—you didn't have to think it out beforehand.

In the case of the short story I was equally misled. It was only the surface of the story which I knew as I began to write—the surprises might not be so far reaching as in a novel, but they were there all the same. They came in the unexpected shaping of a sentence, in a sudden reflection, in an unforeseen flash of dialogue; they came like cool drinks to a parched mouth.

So with this thick volume in front of me I realize that since the beginning I have really been all the time a writer of short stories—they are not the "scraps" I thought them. "The End of the Party" was written in 1929, the year of my first printed novel, and strangely enough, during the period when I was writing my second and third novels, which I have now safely suppressed, I wrote a small story, "I Spy," which has the qualities which all my first novels so disastrously lacked—simplicity of language, the sense of life as it is lived. It is no great thing—"I Spy"—but how, if I were able to write a short story even of that modest truth, could I have been so bent on self-destruction with the total unrealities of *The Name of Action* and *Rumour at Nightfall* (which luckily no one will be able to find today—at least they have escaped what we used to call the sixpenny box)?

Yet, though I am content with many of these stories (I believe I have never written anything better than "The Destructors," "A Chance for Mr. Lever," "Under the Garden," "Cheap in August") I remain in this field a novelist who has happened to write short stories, just as there are certain short story writers (Maupassant and Mr V. S. Pritchett come to mind) who have happened to write novels. This is not a superficial distinction—or even a technical distinction as between an artist who paints in oil or watercolour; it is certainly not a distinction in value. It is a distinction between two different ways of life.

With a novel, which takes perhaps years to write, the author is not the same man at the end of the book as he was at the beginning. It is not only that his characters have developed—he has developed with them, and this nearly always gives a sense of roughness to the work: a novel can seldom have the sense of perfection which you find in Chekhov's story, "The Lady with the Dog." It is the consciousness of that failure which makes the revision of the novel seem endless—the author is trying in vain to adapt the story to his changed personality—as though it were something he had begun in childhood and was finishing now in old age. There are moments of despair when he begins perhaps the fifth revision of Part One, when he sees the multitude of the new corrections. How can he help feeling, "This will never end. I shall never get this passage right"? What he ought to be saying is, "I shall never again be the man I was when I wrote this months and months ago." No wonder that under these conditions a novelist often makes a bad husband or an unstable lover. There is something in his character of the actor who continues to play Othello when he is off the stage, but he is an actor who has lived far too many parts during far too many long runs. He is encrusted with characters. A black taxi driver in the Caribbean once told me of a body which he had seen lifted from the sea. He said, "You couldn't tell it was a man's body because of all the lampreys which came up with it." A horrible image, but it is one which suits the novelist well.

And so the short story for the novelist is often a form of escape—escape from having to live with another character for years on end, picking up his jealousies, his meanness, his dishonest tricks of thought, his betrayals. The reader may well complain of the unpleasantness of the character, but lucky reader! he has only had to spend a few days in his company. Sometimes in Flaubert's letters you can see him becoming Madame Bovary, developing in himself her destructive passion.

This collection therefore can be regarded as a collection of escapes from the novelist's world—even, if you like, of escapades, and I can reread the stories more easily because they do not drag a whole lifetime in their wake. I can look at them quickly as I would look at an album of snapshots taken on many different holidays. Of course they contain memories—sometimes unhappy memories, but if I turn the page, the next picture has no connection with the one before. One book, *May We Borrow Your Husband?*, was indeed written in a single mood of sad hilarity, while I was establishing a home in a two-roomed apartment over the port at Antibes. Taking my dinner nightly, in the little restaurant of Félix au Port, some of the tales emerged from conversations at other tables (even from a phrase misunderstood), though the title story had been in my mind for a number of years. I had brought the idea with me to Antibes as part of my baggage, and I set the scene in Antibes, though in fact I had seen the incident happen under my eyes (or so I imagined) at St Jean-Cap Ferrat while I worked at a hotel window on a very different subject, *A Burnt-Out Case*.

There are other intruders in this particular volume, which otherwise belongs in my mind to one autumn and winter in Antibes. In Kingston, Jamaica, in August, 1963, waiting to obtain a visa for Haiti, I sat over my red snapper and tomatoes watching the monstrous Bermuda shorts go by worn by fat parties from St Louis, and wondered, as my character did, what possible pick-up were possible in this out-of-season hotel. Visitors to Bentley's in Swallow Street may still from time to time observe a gathering of invisible Japanese gentlemen who dine together with a ballet of bows and a glitter of spectacles, and there is one story in this collection called "The Root of All Evil" which does not belong to the same world at all. Set somewhere in the nineteenth century in a provincial German town it belongs, in its crude farce of transvestism and custard-pie, to the free world of dreams—I dreamed the entire story and woke up laughing. I cannot remember changing a single incident, though I suppose there must have been some lacunae which had to be filled in.

Another story which came to me in sleep appears in the collection called *A Sense of Reality*, the story of a leper patient in Sweden who returns to plead with an old medical professor who has condemned him to hospital and finds the house transformed for the night into a gambling casino to please a senile general. I altered only one detail, the revolver shot which coincided with the explosion of the champagne cork. My real dream had faded out on the face of the old general seated at the roulette table. I can still clearly see, as I saw them in sleep, the hired musicians tumbling out of the taxis with their cumbrous instruments. Was I the leper? I think not. I think I was the professor, bemused by the transformation of his house and seeing his patient's face peer in at him from the garden outside.

Dreams, perhaps because I was psycho-analysed as a boy, have always had an importance when I write. The genesis of my novel *It's a Battlefield* was a dream, and a novel which I am working on now began too with a dream. Sometimes identification with a character goes so far that one may dream his dream and not one's own. That happened to me when I was writing *A Burnt-Out Case*. The symbols, the memories, the associations of that dream belonged so clearly to my character Querry that next morning I could put the dream without change into the novel, where it bridged a gap in the narrative which for days I had been unable to cross. I imagine all authors have found the same aid from the unconscious. The unconscious collaborates in all our work: it is a *nègre* we keep in the cellar to aid us. When an obstacle seems insurmountable, I read the day's work before sleep and leave the *nègre* to labour in my place. When I wake the obstacle has nearly always been removed: the solution is there and obvious—perhaps it came in a dream which I have forgotten.

Looking over these stories now which stretch in time from 1929 to the eve of the 1970's I am struck by an odd fact—humour enters very late and very unexpectedly. The only three stories I wrote during the war were humorous ones—there again the short story was an escape, an escape from the blitz and the nightly deaths. So perhaps the stories which make up the collection *May We Borrow Your Husband?*, all written during what should be the last decade of my life, are an escape in humour from the thought of death—this time of certain death. Writing is a form of therapy; sometimes I wonder how all those who do not write, compose or paint can manage to escape the madness, the melancholia, the panic fear which is inherent in the human situation.

Interview with Marie-Françoise Allain

Marie-Françoise Allain: I still do not understand how you associate leprosy and innocence.

Graham Greene: Remember, it was "In the lost boyhood of Judas Christ was betrayed."[1] Judas, finally, was innocent. It was a child's innocence which carried betrayal.

Perhaps I should never have said I felt like a leper but rather like a Quisling (the Norwegian minister who collaborated with the Nazis)—a divided loyalty or the betrayal of one's own loyalty.

In 1959, after three months in the Congo leper colony, I had a dream. I dreamed of a leper in Sweden—yes, Sweden, not Norway. He went to see an old professor of medicine, who shut the door in his face with the advice that he should seek treatment at a clinic. The leper begged him for help; he would lose his job if his disease became public knowledge. The professor replied severely that Swedish law forbade his treating a leper outside a hospital. Then the poor man came back at night and knocked at the Herr Professor's door. And suddenly everything had changed; an officer had turned up in the course of the day and said to the doctor, "Listen, we're giving a party to celebrate the seventieth birthday of our retired general. As Swedish law forbids gambling, we should like to turn your house into a casino just for tonight. It will give the general such a thrill—he used to love playing roulette at Monte Carlo. We'll take care of everything. We'll bring an orchestra, we'll provide the tables, just for the night. The old general will be so pleased!" The professor eventually consented.

So when the leper dragged himself across the fields that night to see the professor and beg him to treat him in secret, the house was totally transformed. There were lights, laughter, cigar smoke. . . . Well, while a champagne cork was gaily popping from a bottle the leper shot

108

himself through the forehead with a revolver. And I've asked myself as I've pondered over this dream of a strange country: "Am I the professor or the leper?"

A little of each I think.

Allain: Once again, a double agent. . . .

Allain: In contrast with writing books, you [as a reporter] proceed on a basis of facts, which is relatively solid in spite of the physical risks, would you not agree?

Greene: There are far more and far subtler risks for a writer. To go to write a news story is something of a holiday for me; a novelist is a creature without scruples, which is tiring. The novelist's station is on the ambiguous borderline between the just and the unjust, between doubt and clarity. But he has to be unscrupulous, as I've already remarked, and I've been misunderstood. I would take Mauriac as an example not to follow. I'm a great admirer of some of his books. But his loyalty to the Catholic church has made him rather too "scrupulous" a writer—in the theological rather than in the moral sense. I expressed this idea in the lecture at Hamburg. A writer must be able to cross over, to "change sides at the drop of a hat. He stands for the victims and the victims change." This obliges him to violate his faith or his political opinions, to be unscrupulous, but it's indispensable. . . .

I aim to be content with what I produce. It's an aim I never achieve, but I go over my work word by word, time and again, so as to be as little dissatisfied as possible. I write not to be read, but for my own relief. My only readership is me. Novelists who write for a public are, in my opinion, no good: They've discovered who their readers are, and, in submitting to their judgment, they're dishing things up like short-order cooks. But a writer has to be his own judge, for his novels contain faults which he alone can discern. The harshest judgments should be his own. . . .

Allain: Your sympathy for the failings in other novelists is surprising, especially in your essays. Should you not have a little more indulgence for your own?

Greene: The writer builds on the foundations of his own deficiencies: A deficiency is often a blessing. The honorary consul, despite his defects, succeeds in loving. He succeeds thanks to his failings. To return to action, I had an unfortunate tendency to encumber it with adjectives and adverbs, which slowed the pace. Nowadays I manage to convey the illusion of action—but I still don't describe it. . . .

Part 2

The "craftsmanlike" aspect of my work is a very conscious one. I pay attention to the "point of view," for instance, and I reread aloud what I have written, making a good number of corrections for the sake of euphony.

On the other hand I've mentioned the character of Minty in *England Made Me*. He was quite a minor character to begin with, but he suddenly asserted himself almost to the point of taking charge. In all my novels I'm content to have blank spaces which I don't know in advance how to fill. The characters are thus able to follow their bent more freely. That's why the novel is, to my mind, more interesting than the short story: The novelist reserves for himself surprises, which he can't afford to do in a very short story which is conceived almost entire before the writing has begun.

When I started to write *Travels with My Aunt*, I didn't expect to be able to finish it. (This is rather unusual, because generally I can at least anticipate a beginning, a middle, and an end.) I'd embarked on this adventure for my own amusement, with no notion of what might happen the next day. A number of ideas I expected to use in short stories became recollections of old Augusta. I was surprised that they all cohered into a logical sequence and that the novel became a finished product, for I'd been regarding it more as an exercise based on the free association of ideas, though I had it clearly in mind that it was to be "a book written for the fun of it . . . the subject is old age and death."

So one shouldn't speak too much of technique or craftsmanship. I place great reliance on what I take to be the unconscious, no doubt because of my experience of psychoanalysis as an adolescent.

This isn't to say that writing is magic; magic does take a hand, though, in little touches—the right element to make the various parts cohere drops into place at the proper time without my realizing it. One has to be borne up by a sort of faith in one's unconscious; one has to maintain good relations with it. One enters into contact with this side of oneself by means of dreams and of those unexpected elements which slip into a novel, and one becomes aware of the role played by the unconscious only at the instant when it materializes, surreptitiously.

Allain: Do you not yourself cultivate this sense of the unreal which these unexpected developments bring about? One has the feeling that your stories are sometimes tales for adults written for your own benefit. I am thinking especially of that strange story in which a sick man returns to the home of his childhood and sees, as he is about to go to sleep, the adventures of the little boy who had gone for a walk "under the garden." What is the meaning of this dream inside a dream about a dream? Is it just a story which you took pleasure in writing?

Greene: Oh, I never "take pleasure in writing"! But I did perhaps free myself temporarily from the tensions of reality, or rather from too realistic a way of writing. No doubt I wanted to go back to my childhood, because the house depicted in "Under the Garden" is similar to the one in which we spent our summer holidays. There was also a pond with an island in the middle—and when I went back many years later, like the narrator in the story, I discovered that there was no need for a raft or a boat to take one across to the island. A jump was all that was needed, for the pond was scarcely bigger than a puddle. The gardener, on the other hand, was still the real gardener. I make the same sort of escape in a passage in *The Human Factor* in which Castle, the adoptive father, tells his son the story of the dragon which hides on the common and only comes out in order to visit him in school.

Allain: Another childhood memory?

Greene: I never knew a dragon, but as a small boy, I knew of plenty of caves which might have been its lair because the common was riddled with trenches dating back to the First World War. Incidentally I nearly broke my neck on several occasions when I went riding on this furrowed common of Berkhamsted.

Allain: These flights into the fantastic, into what you call "fantasy," to which you return, notably in *Doctor Fischer of Geneva*, what do they represent for you?

Greene: I don't really know. Perhaps you're right: I'm escaping. For example, if one can remember an entire dream, the result is a sense of entertainment sufficiently marked to give one the illusion of being catapulted into a different world. One finds oneself remote from one's conscious preoccupations.

Allain: What in your work is the proportion of "entertainment" to these "conscious preoccupations"?

Greene: I really couldn't say. In my earlier books I didn't permit myself many of these flights. The sense of entertainment crops up for the first time in *Stamboul Train*, and more markedly in *England Made Me*, but it doesn't come fully into the open until after 1945. I've noticed, in working on the introductions to the Collected Edition, that all my humorous stories date from the Second World War, as though the proximity of death provoked this irresistible urge to laugh and to "unwind." *Travels with My Aunt* was also written when I was well up in my sixties, in the awareness that I was gradually approaching the wall that does not give way.

Allain: In "Under the Garden" you say that there are two important things in life, "laughter and fear."

Greene: It's not I who say so—it's the narrator, Wilditch. At that time, 1962–63, I probably shared his view, for I was Wilditch as I wrote. Today—I don't know. I'm no longer in the same situation that he was in. He was afraid of dying of cancer, and I'd come out of hospital where I suffered a bronchioscopy after contracting a bad attack of pneumonia, because the doctors thought I might have lung cancer.

When you take note of an aphorism, bear in mind that it expresses the views of the character, which may for that time being coincide with those of the author, but which may be meaningless twenty years later. Nowadays I think that laughter is the important thing, or at least a smile—nothing is worse than a giggle. In fact, I shouldn't speak of laughter so much as of the importance of a certain sense of fun.

Note

1. From "Germinal" by A.E., quoted by Graham Greene in his essay "The Lost Childhood."

An Exchange of Views between Elizabeth Bowen, Graham Greene, and V. S. Pritchett

To Elizabeth Bowen [from Graham Greene]

First I would say there are certain human duties I owe in common with the greengrocer or the clerk—that of supporting my family if I have a family, of not robbing the poor, the blind, the widow or the orphan, of dying if the authorities demand it (it is the only way to remain independent: the conscientious objector is forced to become a teacher in order to justify himself). These are our primitive duties as human beings. In spite of the fashionable example of Gauguin, I would say that if we do less than these, we are so much the less human beings and therefore so much the less likely to be artists. But are there any special duties I owe to my fellow victims bound for the Loire? I would like to imagine there are none, but I fear there are at least two duties the novelist owes—to tell the truth as he sees it and to accept no special privileges from the state.

I don't mean anything flamboyant by the phrase "telling the truth": I don't mean exposing anything. By truth I mean accuracy—it is largely a matter of style. It is my duty to society not to write: "I stood above a bottomless gulf" or "going downstairs, I got into a taxi," because these statements are untrue. My characters must not go white in the face or tremble like leaves, not because these phrases are clichés but because they are untrue. This is not only a matter of the artistic conscience but of the social conscience too. We already see the effect of the popular novel on popular thought. Every time a phrase like one of these passes into the mind uncriticised, it muddies the stream of thought.

The other duty, to accept no privileges, is equally important. The kindness of the State, the State's interest in art, is far more dangerous than its indifference. We have seen how in time of war there is always some well-meaning patron who will suggest that artists should be in

Excerpted and reprinted from *Why Do I Write?* (Percival Marshall, 1948), 29–32, 47–49. Reprinted with permission of William Heinemann, Ltd. and The Bodley Head, Ltd.

113

a reserved class. But how, at the end of six years of popular agony, would the artist be regarded if he had been reserved, kept safe and fattened at the public expense, too good to die like other men? And what would have been expected of him in return? In Russia, the artist *has* belonged to a privileged class: he has been given a better flat, more money, more food, even a certain freedom of movement: but the State has asked in return that he should cease to be an artist. The danger does not exist only in totalitarian countries. The bourgeois state, too, has its gifts to offer to the artist—or those it regards as artists, but in these cases the artist has paid like the politician in advance. One thinks of the literary knights, and then one turns to the plain tombstones with their bare *hic jacets* of Mr. Hardy, Mr. James and Mr. Yeats. Yes, the more I think of it, that is a duty the artist unmistakably owes to society—to accept no favours. Perhaps a pension if his family are in danger of starvation (in those circumstances the moralists admit that we may commit theft).

Perhaps the greatest pressure on the writer comes from the society within society: his political or his religious group, even it may be his university or his employers. It does seem to me that one privilege he can claim, in common perhaps with his fellow human beings, but possibly with greater safety, is that of disloyalty. I met a farmer at lunch the other day who was employing two lunatics; what fine workers they were, he said; and how loyal. But, of course, they were loyal; they were like the conditioned beings of the brave new world. Disloyalty is our privilege. But it is a privilege you will never get society to recognise. All the more necessary that we who can be disloyal with impunity should keep that ideal alive.

If I may be personal, I belong to a group, the Catholic Church, which would present me with grave problems as a writer if I were not saved by my disloyalty. If my conscience were as acute as M. Mauriac's showed itself to be in his essay *God and Mammon*, I could not write a line. There are leaders of the Church who regard literature as a means to one end, edification. That end may be of the highest value, of far higher value than literature, but it belongs to a different world. Literature has nothing to do with edification. I am not arguing that literature is amoral, but that it presents a personal moral, and the personal morality of an individual is seldom identical with the morality of the group to which he belongs. You remember the black and white squares of Bishop Blougram's chess board. As a novelist, I must be allowed to write from the point of view of the black square as well as of the white: doubt and even denial must be given their chance of self-expression, or how is one freer than the Leningrad group? . . .

To V. S. Pritchett [from Graham Greene]

Here in parenthesis I would emphasise once again the importance and the virtue of disloyalty. If only writers could maintain that one virtue— so much more important to them than purity—unspotted from the world. Honours, State patronage, success, the praise of their fellows all tend to sap their disloyalty. If they don't become loyal to a Church or a country, they are too apt to become loyal to some invented ideology of their own, until they are praised for consistency, for a unified view. Even despair can become a form of loyalty. How few die treacherous or blaspheming in old age, and have any at all been lucky enough to die by the rope or a firing squad? I can think of none, for the world knows only too well that given time the writer will be corrupted into loyalty. Ezra Pound therefore goes to an asylum . . . (the honourable haven of the uncorruptible—Smart, Cowper, Clare and Lee). Loyalty confines us to accepted opinions: loyalty forbids us to comprehend sympathetically our dissident fellows; but disloyalty encourages us to roam experimentally through any human mind: it gives to the novelist the extra dimension of sympathy.

I hope I have made it clear that I am not advocating a conscious advocacy of the dispossessed, in fact I am not advocating propaganda at all, as it was written by Dickens, Charles Reade or Thomas Hood. The very act of re-creation for the novelist entails sympathy: the characters for whom he fails in sympathy have never been truly re-created. Propaganda is only concerned to elicit sympathy for the innocent, or those whom the propagandist likes to regard as innocent, and this he does at the expense of the guilty: he too poisons the wells. But the novelist's task is to draw his own likeness to any human being, the guilty as much as the innocent. Isn't our attitude to all our characters more or less—There, and may God forgive me, goes myself?

If we can awaken sympathetic comprehension in our readers, not only for our most evil characters (that is easy: there is a cord there fastened to all hearts that we can twitch at will), but of our smug, complacent, successful characters, we have surely succeeded in making the work of the State a degree more difficult—and that is a genuine duty we owe society, to be a piece of grit in the State machinery. However acceptable the Soviet State may at the moment find the great classic writers, Dostoevski, Tolstoy, Chekhov, Turgenev, Gogol, they have surely made the regimentation of the Russian spirit an imperceptible degree more difficult or more incomplete. You cannot talk of the Karamazovs in terms of a class, and if you speak with hatred of the kulak doesn't the rich humorous memory of the hero of *Dead Souls* come back to kill your hatred? Sooner or later the strenuous note of social responsibility, of Marxism, of the greatest material good of the greatest number must die in the ear, and then perhaps certain memories will come back, of long purposeless discussions in the moonlight about life and art, the click of a billiard ball, the sunny afternoons of that month in the country, the blows of an axe that has only just begun to fell the cherry trees.

I am sorry to return over and over again to this question of loyalty or disloyalty, but isn't disloyalty as much the writer's virtue as loyalty is the soldier's? For the writer, just as much as the Christian Church, is the defender of the individual. The soldier, the loyal man, stands for the mass interment, the common anonymous grave, but the writer stands for the uneconomic, probably unhealthy, overcrowded little graveyard, with the stone crosses preserving innumerable names.

Part 3

THE CRITICS

Introduction

Graham Greene's short fiction has received little critical attention. Nearly all of the studies that have appeared during the past five decades focus upon his novels. Although he has written short stories, plays, travel books, poetry, film criticism, film scripts, book reviews, and biography, Greene remains first and foremost a novelist. Nevertheless, the critical response to his work is out of balance, ignoring as it has his achievements in these other areas. Some recent studies of Greene and the cinema, however, are beginning to address that imbalance. I hope that this study and the essays that follow will not only demonstrate Greene's achievements as a writer of short fiction but provide new insights into the evolution of themes and techniques that shape his work in other genres.

I have included Gwenn Boardman's essay for its recognition of the seminal mythic themes contained in Greene's "Under the Garden." It is one of the first thorough critical discussions of a Greene short story and demonstrates the mythic themes that unify his works in other genres. A. R. Coulthard's essay serves to question and possibly correct the simple, straightforward reading of the frequently anthologized "The Hint of an Explanation." Coulthard reminds the reader that Greene is a skillful ironist and that his stories may yield several interpretations. John Ower's analysis of "The Destructors" demonstrates the centripetal nature of the story by examining the complex development of themes from psychology, sociology, history, and theology.

A. R. Coulthard

Good fiction, as the saying goes, lends itself to a number of interpretations. But a generation of readers brought up on irony, ambiguity, and levels of meaning has been uncharacteristically eager to accept Graham Greene's widely anthologized "The Hint of an Explanation" as merely a simple moral drama and enthusiastically to praise it as such.

On the surface, the story *is* simple. A chance traveling companion of a priest retells a story that the priest told him while on a train trip. There is little dramatic interplay between the priest and the narrator. The traveler's retelling of the priest's story is objective, consisting almost entirely of a restatement of the priest's own words.

The priest is as subjective as the narrator is objective, and herein lies the problem of a one-level interpretation. The cleric not only tells the story, but explains its meaning to his fellow traveler. If the reader accepts the priest's interpretation of his childhood experience, the story is elementary. Its theme is that God sends saving signs, or hints, to his chosen. These hints of God's power often come in the form of evil which, with God's help, the tempted resists and eventually thwarts.

As his name suggests, Blacker is ostensibly the embodiment of evil in the story. When the priest was a young altar boy, Blacker, by threats and bribery, persuaded him to steal a consecrated wafer from his church. Blacker supposedly wanted the wafer for evil purposes. However, just as he was about to lay hands on it, the boy found the strength and courage to foil him by swallowing it down. As a mature adult, the priest sees this event as the turning point in his life. Foiling Blacker convinced the boy of God's power to defeat evil and eventually led him into the priesthood.

The temptation is to accept the priest as Greene's spokesman and regard his interpretation as the one that the reader is supposed to share. But such a simple reading of the story raises several questions. Should

Reprinted from "Graham Greene's 'The Hint of an Explanation': A Reinterpretation," *Studies in Short Fiction* 8 (Fall 1971): 601–5. Reprinted by permission of *Studies in Short Fiction*, Newberry College.

the reader uncritically accept the priest's interpretation of an experience in which he is obviously quite emotionally involved—an experience which, in effect, his entire life rests upon? Is the priest, simply because he is a priest, immune from error? William E. Buckler and Arnold B. Sklare seem willing to take the priest at his word:

> In the priest's apologia, the hint of an explanation stems from living proof that infinite good may rise out of abysmal evil. Blacker is clearly an embodiment of black evil—he deliberately chooses to trap a child barely beyond the age of reason into sinning against himself and God. But the boy, by his capacity to resist, is for the first time able to understand good. This happiness launches him on his religious life, for he has begun to sense the power of God—how God works and the nature of life. His self-realization in the priesthood—his recognition of God—is the infinite good through God which has resulted from his encounter with the diabolical man. . . .[1]

However, if the reader chooses to interpret for himself the meaning of the priest's story (as the traveling companion, an agnostic, seems tacitly to do), he might arrive at an explication quite different from that of the priest (and Greene himself?). First of all, there is the problem of Blacker's character. Although the obvious label name tends to stack the deck against him, the fact is that Blacker doesn't seem all that black. Even in the priest's biased account, Blacker seems at least as much sinned against as sinning. The priest admits that although Blacker was one of only two bakers in the town, "I don't think any of the Catholics patronized him because he was a free-thinker." And if the priest considers the baker's "one wall eye and a head the shape of a turnip, with the hair gone on the crown" to be outward signs of inward evil, the gentle reader might merely deem Blacker's ugliness all the more reason to pity him. Certainly Blacker's ugliness and reputation for "free-thinking" do not justify the Catholics' excluding him from their community of worship. But the priest says, with complete aplomb, "It would have been no good, you understand, in a little town like that, presenting himself for communion. Everybody there knew him for what he was." Quite opposite a demonic hatred of good, Blacker has valid reasons for disliking the Catholics of the community.

A second interpretive problem concerns Blacker's motives: The priest assumes them to have been totally and simply evil: "That poor man was preparing to revenge himself on everything he hated—my father, the Catholics, the God whom people persisted in crediting—

and that by corrupting me." Let us ignore the egotism of this statement for the moment and examine the possibility that the priest mistakes Blacker's motives—that Blacker, because of his ostracism, could not with self-respect express an interest in Catholicism and that what the priest regards as Blacker's diabolical scheme was really his clumsy attempt to reach out for God. Blacker was familiar with the Catholic doctrine of transubstantiation and seems to have been struggling with it. In the priest's account, Blacker feigns cynicism to the boy by saying, "I can bake the things you eat [wafers at Mass] just as well as any Catholic can," but he immediately gives himself away by blurting "with sudden intensity, 'how I'd like to get one of your ones in my mouth—just to see. . . .' " It is at this point that Blacker persuades the boy to agree to steal a consecrated wafer for him. Blacker's statement, "I want to see what your God tastes like," has the ring of a sincere, if grotesque, interest in communion.

As Blacker instructs his young accomplice, the boy is surprised at how well the free-thinker knows the routine of Catholic Mass. "How carefully he had been studying the ground," the priest comments later. "He must have slipped several times into Mass at the back of the church." But, surprisingly, it does not occur to the priest that a knowledge of the ritual of Mass would have been of no use to Blacker in stealing a wafer and that maybe Blacker had slipped into the back of the church to worship. This interpretation is given weight by the fact that just as the boy is about to steal the wafer, he sees Blacker "watching from the back of the church. He had put on his best black Sunday clothes." Surely if Blacker were the blasphemer the priest makes him out to have been, he would not have felt compelled to dress appropriately before entering the church.

Later that night, Blacker furtively came to the boy's home to fetch his hard-earned wafer. Intentionally or not, Blacker is depicted in decidedly sympathetic terms in this last scene. The boy hears Blacker's whistle and opens the curtains to find him in an attitude of supplication: "If I had reached my hand down, his fingers reaching up could almost have touched mine." Symbolically, Blacker is reaching out for some form of human communion, for something to cling to and dispel the meaninglessness of his life. But the boy does not reach back. Instead, in a moment of what he later considers to have been divine inspiration, he swallows the wafer in order to keep it from Blacker. Then Blacker, that archvillain and agent of the Fiend, that miscreant who had promised the boy that he would slit his throat if he failed to cooperate, "began to weep—the tears ran lopsidedly out of the one good eye and his shoulders shook."

As a mature adult looking back on this incident, the priest, instead of feeling compassion for Blacker, sees the whole affair as a sort of moral allegory designed for his own benefit. "When I think of it now, it's almost as if I had seen the Thing weeping for its inevitable defeat," he says. The agnostic, who serves the dual dramatic purpose of listener and, later, narrator of the priest's story, is not so sure. "It's an interesting story," he tells the priest. "I think I should have given Blacker what he wanted." When the agnostic wonders aloud what Blacker would have done with the wafer, the priest's response is superstitious and vague—almost, it may strike the reader, ignorant: "I really believe that he would first of all have put it under his microscope—before he did all the other things I expect he had planned."

As has been suggested, the priest is so wrapped up in what the experience did for him that he virtually ignores what it did *to* Blacker. The agnostic's parting remark to the priest may be intended as an ironic suggestion. "I suppose you think you owe a lot to Blacker," he says. "Yes," replies the priest, "you see I am a very happy man."

In attempting to explain just what Graham Greene intended to communicate in this story, two possibilities arise. The first is that, as Buckler and Sklare and other critics suggest, the priest's interpretation of the experience should be taken at face value. Implicit in this interpretation is the premise that, in effect, the priest speaks for the author and that Greene's intention and the priest's interpretation are one and the same. If this be the case, then the story is weak artistically, because it forces an interpretation upon the reader, and dialectically, because Greene asks the reader to believe that God would save one man by destroying another.

Another possibility, however, is that Greene intended for the discerning reader to weigh the priest's conclusions against the facts contained in his own account. If priest's and reader's conclusions do not agree, then the story may be seen as an understated satire on a proud, complacent priest who deigns to believe that God, for all His infinite mercy, would lead him into the priesthood by having him trod down a helpless, pitiable creature such as Blacker. In this interpretation the story is enriched by the unconscious irony of the priest's account.

Several elements in the story point to this second interpretation. Blacker lacks the power of the conventional villain, and Greene constantly plays off the priest's complacency against Blacker's helplessness. For example, juxtaposed with the pathetic picture of Blacker's abject misery over his failure to obtain the wafer is the priest's puffy statement, "you see, *I* am a very happy man" [my italics]. The priest's sense of superiority over Blacker pervades the story. If Greene had favored the priest's point of view, surely he would have depicted his protagonist more sympathetically. Moreover, Greene's choice of an agnostic as the priest's audience invites a skeptical look at the priest. One can't help but wonder how the priest's story strikes this uncommitted listener.

Adding to the irony of the priest's conclusions is the fact that even he seems to sense that he might have been wrong about Blacker. He admits, for example, that Blacker's nature "did contain, perhaps, a certain furtive love." Recalling how Blacker, "looking so longingly and pleadingly" up at him, tried to coax the wafer from him by saying "It's only a piece of bread," the priest muses: "even as a child I wondered whether he could really think that, and yet desire it so much." But the priest has too much at stake to dwell long on such misgivings.

If Greene had intended for the reader to share the priest's interpretation of his childhood experience, would he have thrown so many obstacles in the way of that interpretation? Two inescapable facts of the story are that Blacker was a man cut off from both God and humanity and that both as a boy and as an adult, the priest responded with a singular lack of compassion. Greene's story, therefore, may be read as a "hint" to complacent Christians that one of Jesus' best known teachings, "Inasmuch as you did it to the least of these, my brethren, you did it unto me," is a two-sided coin.

Note

1. From *Stories from Six Authors*, edited by William E. Buckler and Arnold B. Sklare. (New York: McGraw-Hill, 1960).

John Ower

Graham Greene's "The Destructors" is one of the minor masterpieces of modern fiction. Within its narrow compass, Greene incorporates a comprehensive vision, which embraces psychology, sociology, history and theology.[1] The remarkable scope of his story permits a complex analysis of the many-headed crisis of modern culture.

Historically, "The Destructors" traces the spiritual and cultural disintegration of Europe from the late Eighteenth Century onwards. The climax of this dissolution, the Second World War, provides the immediate background of Greene's story. The Wormsley Common Gang inhabit a heavily bombed area of London. Not only does their delinquency reflect the psychological shock and the social disintegration which accompany war, but there is an obvious comparison of Trevor with Hitler, of his gang with the Nazis. Like Camus in *The Rebel*,[2] and Ionesco in *Rhinoceros*, Greene sees Nazism as a form of nihilism, which reacts to a world stripped of value and meaning with an answering outburst of violence. Greene also recalls the existentialist writers in attributing this spiritual crisis to three major factors: the historical breakdown of absolute values, a sense of the alienness and indifference of the universe, and an acute awareness of man's time-bound nature.

The final collapse of absolutes in our time is attributed by Greene to the crumbling during the previous two centuries of the spiritual authority of Christianity. That its values once provided the foundation of European culture is suggested by the Thomas house, which was designed by the famous architect of St. Paul's Cathedral. Conversely, the destruction of the house indicates that, without the Church as a moral centre, civilization itself will fall. Whatever its failings, the Christianity which was institutionalized into the old order at least fostered the charity and the self-restraint which are essential to human community. It encouraged the spirit of kindness, forgiveness and

Reprinted from "Dark Parable: History and Theology in Graham Greene's 'The Destructors,'" *Cithara* 15 (November 1975): 69–78. Reprinted by permission of *Cithara*.

generosity displayed in Thomas' gift of candy to the gang. More generally, Greene sees Christianity as underlying the traditional British sense of decency and fair-play. If the gang is willing to respect Mr. Thomas' privacy, and to recognize that his house is his castle, he will allow them the occasional use of his "lav." Such give and take, based upon charity, fairness and mutual respect, is essential to a viable society.

That Wren at once engaged in sacred and domestic architecture implies that Christianity has also been responsible for a beauty and a decorum which ordered and elevated the whole of daily life. This union of the aesthetic and the utilitarian is epitomized in the spiral staircase in Thomas' house. The stair, which is supported by the balance of "opposite forces,"[3] suggests a Yeatsian vision of culture as a balance and reconciliation of contraries in a "ceremony of innocence." The stair also represents the use of intellect and of technology for the creation of beauty rather than for wanton destruction. It is opposed to the chaos and the ugliness of the modern world, which are appropriately symbolized by the pile of rubble to which the house is finally reduced.

"The Destructors" thus suggests that Greene is projecting into the past an ideal state of culture, in which the predominance of Christianity ensures both refinement and order. His reference to Wren indicates that he sees the early Eighteenth Century, with its relatively stable social structure, its well entrenched values, and its polished urbanity, as the last period of constructive civilization in Europe. The obvious corollary of this position, that the Romantic era represents a "fall" which paves the way for the contemporary crisis, is also central to "The Destructors." Just as the positive culture of the Augustan Age is symbolized by the Thomas house, so its destroyer T. embodies Romantic negativity. For example, the oft-mentioned connection between German Romanticism and Nazism is implied by T.'s demonic parody of Nietzsche's *uebermensch*.[4] Like the "overman," T. is an intellectually superior individual, with a superabundance of the "will-to-power." He has in his own satanic way "transvalued" the values of the past, and ruthlessly imposes his "superior" purpose on lesser mortals.

Greene's attack upon Romantic hero-worship is, however, directed chiefly at Byron.[5] T. resembles the Byronic hero in being an exceptional individual, an "aristocrat" by virtue of both his social origins and his superior gifts. He dominates his fellows through his intellectual attainments, his personal aura, and his dark spiritual energy. Although a born leader, T. follows his Byronic prototype in remaining an individualist, a renegade, and an anarchist. He is aloof, brooding and self-contained, an alienated outcast from civilization who is in revolt against its moral and spiritual authority.

In true Byronic fashion, T.'s rebelliousness also involves a Luciferian rejection of God. Thus, in destroying the house, he wilfully courts damnation. His awareness of the wickedness of his scheme is apparent even when he first proposes it to the gang. Ashamed to reveal his dark purpose, he stands apart, staring at his feet. T.'s deliberate evil is underscored by his celebration of a "Black Mass" in burning Thomas' savings, a piece of cold-blooded satanism which is all the worse because it is calculated to implicate Blackie. This travesty of Communion suggests that T. is completely cut off from either man or God by his self-absorption in his own evil.

One of the crimes for which the Byronic hero is damned is incest,[6] and this indirectly throws light upon T.'s motivation for destroying the house. In Freudian theory, incest expresses the child's Oedipal desire to kill his father and to possess his mother. The preoccupation of Romanticism with incest can therefore be related to its leitmotif of revolt against the father, and against authority-figures in general. T.'s destruction of the house illustrates this Oedipal-Romantic syndrome. His normal adolescent rebelliousness is accentuated by feelings of betrayal and humiliation arising from his father's social and economic failure. Because his parent has been an architect, to destroy a beautiful building is symbolically to murder him. The value of the Thomas house as a focus for T.'s Oedipal hatred is reinforced by its owner's fatherly gesture in giving the gang candy, and by his previous employment as a "builder and decorator" (p. 328). At the same time, the bomb-damaged structure may represent for T. the tottering moral, social and spiritual order, which is analogous to a weak paternal authority. In particular, through its association with St. Paul's, the house may be the symbol of a God whose apparent failure to save society must seem to T. to repeat his father's dereliction.

In rebelling against his father, T. copies him by way of reaction. The father is an architect; T. is a "destructor." The older man is a failure while his son, apart from a momentary faltering of his authority, is a strong and successful leader. T.'s "reverse imitation" of his parent indicates that he is bound up in a love-hate relationship with him. His revolt may therefore be a perverse expression of a desire for a strong father and, by extension, for God's saving power and for an effective social authority.

As a social and a metaphysical rebel, isolated and even damned by his egoism and wickedness, the Byronic hero epitomizes the upheaval which characterized every aspect of the Romantic age. The period therefore marks the real beginning of the collapse of absolutes and of order which culminates in the Twentieth Century. However, the human type which is the end-product of this destructive process is thoroughly unromantic. Such a modern Everyman is the truck-driver who appropriately if unwittingly completes the demolition of Thomas' house. Like the gang-members, the driver has been coarsened and even brutalized by the deficiencies and the enormities of his world. His cruel laughter at the havoc which he has created suggests that contemporary man is not simply alienated from his heritage, but hates it and wishes to see it destroyed. The driver is incapable even of the elementary human concern which should move him to respond to Thomas' cries of distress. He ironically underlines his own inhumanity by his plea that there is "nothing personal" (p. 346) in his amusement at the collapse of the house. His extenuation also implies the child's indiscriminate joy in destruction, untrammeled by any civilizing influences. It is to such neo-barbarism, typified by the fascist bully-boy, that Byronism has finally degenerated.

However, T.'s demolition of the Wren house sums up more than the previous two centuries of European history. For Greene, their catastrophic climax is a particularly extreme outbreak of an evil which is larger than man and his annals. Thus, T.'s rebellion against God recalls that of Lucifer. The boy who has never been a child is age-old, a type and embodiment of the destructive presence of the Devil in both humanity and nature. The cosmic scope of this malificence is suggested in "The Destructors" by storm-imagery. On the Sunday when the wrecking begins, "The tired evergreens kept off a stormy sun: another wet Bank Holiday was being prepared over the Atlantic" (p. 335). The potential of nature for violence is connected to that in man by Greene's comparison of the thunder to "the first guns of the old blitz" (p. 338). Similarly, when T. initially proposes that the house be destroyed, his eyes are "as grey and disturbed as the drab August day" (p. 332).

Greene's storm-imagery suggests that the effect of evil in man and nature is to counteract God's creative power; to attack the order which He made and pronounced good. This idea is crystallized in the description of the gang's destructive work: "*Chaos* had advanced. . . . *Streaks of light* came in through the closed shutters where they worked with the seriousness of *creators*—and destruction after all is a form of creation" (pp. 336–337; italics mine). This studied symbolic parody of the opening chapter of Genesis is reinforced by the inception of the gang's work on the Sabbath, the day on which God rested after having made the world (Genesis 2:1–3). Greene is playing here on the root meaning of the word "holiday." The August Bank Holiday weekend, which should be a time of innocent recreation for body and spirit, is profaned by the destructive presence of evil in both man and nature.

The subversion of humanity by Satan began with the temptation of Adam and Eve. Their lapse is alluded to in T.'s statement that, in destroying the house from within, the gang would work like "worms . . . in an apple" (p. 332).[7] T.'s takeover of the gang for his sinister purposes thus repeats the Fall. This recapitulation of "man's first disobedience" suggests the doctrine of original sin. Because Adam and Eve defied God, the human race has to some extent become both the victim and the agent of Satan's malignity. It follows that, despite the alleviations of religion and culture, history is unavoidably tragic. The suffering and dereliction of fallen man are indicated by Thomas' nickname of "Old Misery," which appropriately recalls the Devil's affliction of Job.

The fallen state of nature and humanity is responsible for the two "existential" problems of an alien universe and of man's bondage to time and death. Thus Old Misery, sitting helplessly imprisoned in his "lav" as the gang wrecks his house, becomes aware of the cold and even malicious indifference of the world to human suffering: "Mr. Thomas tried one more yell, but he was daunted and rebuked by the silence—a long way off an owl hooted and made away again on its muffled flight through the soundless world" (p. 345). The hooting of the owl suggests the mocking of man's feelings by the power of evil that silently perpetrates its ravages in nature. The same cosmic derision is implied by Thomas' horoscope, which predicts his misfortune accurately, but in "parables and double meanings" (p. 343) so that he is unable to prevent it.

The theme of man's subjection to time and death also centres upon Thomas. It is suggested by his nickname and by his "rheumatics" (p. 345). It is likewise implied by the sorry figure that he cuts as he limps home in the rain from his spoiled holiday. His mud-caked shoes indicate the origin of man's mortality in the Fall by recalling God's curse of death upon Adam: "dust thou art, and unto dust shalt thou return" (Genesis 3:19). The words of Genesis also underline the sinister significance of Thomas' "lav," which stands "like a tomb in a neglected graveyard" (p. 335). The pit of an outdoor privy is a perfect symbol of man's eventual return to the "dust" through the corruption of his flesh. Old Misery, imprisoned with the smell of his mortality in his upright coffin, is therefore an apt image of our carnal bondage to the fatal ravages of time.

The intensification of modern man's awareness of time and death by his materialistic outlook is suggested in the burning of Thomas' savings by T. and Blackie: ". . . taking it in turns they held a note upwards and lit the top corner, *so that the flame burnt slowly towards their fingers.* The *grey ash* floated above them and fell on their heads *like age* (pp. 337–338; italics mine). Greene's reference to the Ash Wednesday service again recalls God's curse upon Adam. This is ironically related to modern positivism by a further allusion to Christ's injunction to lay up one's treasures in Heaven, "where neither moth nor rust doth corrupt, and where thieves do not break through nor steal" (Matthew 6:20). The connection between materialism and a painful awareness of time and death is also made through the parody of the Mass in the burning of Thomas' savings, which involves a sort of reverse transubstantiation. The spiritual food of Christ's body, which gives eternal life, is contrasted with the fate of Adam's clay as it is suggested by the grey ash, and by the threat of scorched fingers. Similarly, T.'s assertion after the holocaust that "There's only things" (p. 338) is linked to a melancholy consciousness of mortality when he glances around the room "crowded with the unfamiliar shadows of half things, broken things, former things" (p. 338).

The burning of Thomas' savings thus indicates that the root of modern man's destructive nihilism is his sense of entrapment by time. In this regard, Greene draws an ironic contrast between men and material objects which recalls Sartre's distinction between the "pour-soi" and the "en-soi."[8] T. is right in asserting that in a world of things, our emotions would be "hooey" (p. 338), but he forgets that a human being is not a mere object. Rather, man is a self-conscious subject, with an acute awareness of his own destiny. He therefore cannot submit passively and indifferently to time as can a simple thing. Without the consolations of religion, he reacts to his death-sentence with deep feelings of outrage and betrayal. T. is typical of contemporary man in that he paradoxically rebels against the pain and the absurdity of his lot by becoming their agent. He is not merely the victim of time's destructiveness, but also furthers it himself.

However, the havoc created by T. not only reflects the consequences of the Fall, but also looks forward to the Apocalypse, when God will destroy a corrupt world to make way for "a new heaven and a new earth" (Revelations 21:1). The eschatological significance of T.'s mayhem is underlined by allusions to two other Biblical episodes which prefigure the last days. Thus, in the early stages of the demolition, T. warns Mike not to prematurely cause a "flood" (p. 336) by turning on the taps. Similarly, the Blitz recalls God's obliteration of Sodom and Gomorrah with a rain of fire and brimstone (Genesis 19:24–25). In all three cases, the Divinity renews the order of Creation by overturning it to annihilate evil. As a "destructor," T. may therefore be not simply a minister of Satan. He could also be an agent of divine retribution and redemption, a destroying angel like those who visit Sodom (Genesis 19) or wreck the universe at the Apocalypse (Revelations 8–9).

Greene's reference to the Apocalypse is therefore ambiguous, suggesting both Fall and Redemption, good and evil, destruction and renewal. It implies that even his view of the modern world is not completely bleak. Thus, there are a number of indications of redemptive grace in "The Destructors." The boy Summers, looking into the pit of rubble which the gang has created, wonders "with astonishment" (p. 339) why the ravage ever began. He relents further at the news of Thomas' unexpected return, suggesting that the wrecking should cease because "We've done enough anyway" (p. 339). His reactions imply that a relative loss of innocence can involve a corresponding growth in moral awareness. Redemption is also suggested negatively in Greene's story through references to Christ's Passion. For example, the first tools for which T. calls in organizing the destruction of the house are "some big nails. . . . and a hammer" (p. 334).[9]

The theme of salvation is centered in "The Destructors" upon the equivocal figure of Mike. He is younger than the rest of the gang and, despite his participation in its delinquency, has retained his innocence. The spirit of child's play with which he approaches even the destruction of the house paradoxically indicates that vestiges of Eden still remain amidst the contemporary crisis. However, Mike's insouciance also suggests the ambiguity of his innocence in a fallen world. Not only is he incapable of withstanding the evil represented by T., but he is essentially amoral. Mike is below an awareness of good and evil, and he can engage in wrong-doing without a qualm.

However, Mike's innocence is reinforced by what remains of the redemptive order of Church and society. As the play of his name upon the slang-term "Mick" indicates, the child is an Irish Catholic. He therefore belongs to a religion which maintains definite standards of discipline and order, such as the obligation to attend the Sunday service. That the command to go to Mass comes through his father implies how the regulation of his Church is confirmed, albeit ineffectively, by the authority of the family. It is possible that, however weakened the traditional system to which Mike belongs, it can still save him.

The divinely ordained dispensation in which Mike at least nominally participates is suggested by his heavenly namesake. As the chief of the angelic hierarchy, Michael is an appropriate symbol of God's authority and order. This is particularly true because the Archangel played a major role in the defeat of Satan's insurrection. However, as Mike's subversion by T. and the gang implies, the initial triumph of divine governance appears to be reversed in a fallen world. The symbolic victory of Satan over Michael is nonetheless temporary. The eventual restoration of God's authority is suggested in terms particularly appropriate to the Satan-Michael antithesis by the angels of the Apocalypse, who help to destroy a corrupt creation, and to rout the Devil and his forces (Revelations 20: 1–3).

However, in a fallen world, order can be the instrument of evil as well as of redemption, an ambivalence which is evident in the Wormsley Common Gang. The gang is in part a desperate attempt to hedge against the surrounding chaos, to replace the very polity that it helps to destroy. Thus, the gang has an elaborate set of rules, and a leader to enforce them. Its spirit of regulation is embodied in Blackie who, in keeping with his office, is the perfect organization-man. Blackie is governed by an impartial sense of justice, and has a strong attachment to duty and procedure. He is not only concerned with the enforcement of the rules, but tends to be limited by them in his outlook. He is a cautious, level-headed pragmatist, always anticipating possible dangers and practical difficulties. Moreover, Blackie is so concerned about the gang's public image that, after his deposition by T., he goes along with the exploit proposed by his rival because of the notice which it will attract. Blackie's dream that "The fame of the . . . gang . . . (will) reach around London," winning the respect of adult mobsters and making "headlines in the papers" (p. 333), sums up the contradictory position of himself and his peers. Although a rebel against the social order, Blackie is deeply sympathetic with its aims, and desires its recognition.

However, in the last analysis, the organization of the gang merely increases its anti-social potential. This point is recognized by T., who rules its members far more strictly than Blackie has done. In the demolition of the house, the "old happy-go-lucky ways" (p. 333) are replaced by a tightly disciplined effort. T.'s regime thus illustrates the tragic paradox that, in a fallen world, order can itself be subverted to the ends of anarchy. Greene ironically underlines this anomaly when Blackie steps in to save T.'s leadership. T.'s rescue to complete his destructive work by the level-headed bureaucrat, represents the final perversion of order by evil.

Because T.'s relationship to order is purely negative, he is beyond its redemptive potential. He is nevertheless offered salvation, although in a form appropriate to the extreme crisis that he represents. T.'s "radical" experience of grace, which occurs when he temporarily loses his hold upon the gang, resembles that of Pinkie in *Brighton Rock*. God approaches T. "between the saddle and the ground," in a moment of painful failure which at once epitomizes his spiritual dereliction, and unites him with the final agony of Christ crucified. T.'s instant of grace is thus an *askesis*. By shattering the previous pattern of his life, and by driving home his fallible mortality, it might have humbled him and restored him to the human community. Appropriately enough, however, T. is "saved" to seal his own damnation by the boy he has initiated into Satanism through his Black Mass. Greene may intend this ironic twist to echo Christ's terrible warning to the corruptors of innocence (Matthew 18: 6–7).

In its complex development of its themes, "The Destructors" provides a fine example of "enveloping action," of the implicit connection of a story with larger historical and spiritual movements which enlarge its significance. In this regard, Greene's story is thematically structured like a "chinese box." The gang's destruction of the house grows from the mayhem of the Second World War, which is in turn the culmination of the moral and social collapse of Europe from the late Eighteenth Century onwards. Finally, the historical "fall" of the West is related to the larger pattern of Salvation History. This extends from the rebellion of Lucifer, through the Creation and the Fall, to Redemption and Apocalypse. That Greene is able to achieve such thematic richness in a piece of short fiction indicates his mastery of the symbolic theological parable as a means of artistic communication.

Notes

1. For a brief discussion of the story, including an analysis of the theme of class conflict, see Laurence J. Perrine, *Instructor's Manual for Literature: Structure, Sound, and Sense* (New York: Harcourt Brace, 1974), pp. 5–6.

2. Camus, *The Rebel* (London: Hamish Hamilton, 1954), p. 149.

3. See Graham Greene, *Collected Stories* (London: The Bodley Head, 1972), p. 331. All quotations are uniform with this edition, to which page-numbers in parentheses refer.

4. For a succinct discussion of Nietzsche's "overman," see Frederick Copleston, *A History of Philosophy*, vol. 7, part II (New York: Doubleday, 1965). p. 188.

5. See Peter Thorslev, *The Byronic Hero* (Minneapolis: University of Minnesota Press, 1962).

6. I am thinking here specifically of Byron's Manfred.

7. The idea of the serpent in Eden as a worm is echoed in the name "Wormsley Common Gang."

8. For a brief discussion of this matter, see Maurice Cranston, *Sartre* (Edinburgh: Oliver and Boyd, 1970), pp. 43–44.

9. A further indication of God's redemptive grace which would be apparent to any Londoner is that, although the Germans heavily damaged the district around St. Paul's, and tried to bomb the cathedral itself, the structure escaped major damage.

Gwenn R. Boardman

"Under the Garden," first published in Greene's *A Sense of Reality* (1963), might well have been written as a commentary on his own explorations, his aesthetic discoveries that have invariably been tied to actual journeys, whether to Africa, Mexico, or Indo-China. It is a mythic rendition of his recurrent themes of lost childhood, of a universal "journey without maps," and a quest for "the heart of the matter." As counterpoint to these thematic variations, there are echoes of familiar episodes, characters, and symbols from Greene's other writing.

As far back as 1936, Greene wrote of ". . . legend, figures which will dramatize the deepest personal fantasy and deepest moral consciousness of a man's time: this . . . is the only thing worth attempting." In "Under the Garden" he has provided his own form of legend and figures (Javitt and Maria) who do indeed dramatize both personal fantasy and moral consciousness. This fifty-nine page story could serve also as a commentary on Greene's theory and practice of the craft of fiction. At first the reader may see little evidence of the questing artist in a boy's record of exploring a dark passage with hieroglyphics on its wall. Rather than tracing a path to the creative process, Wilditch appears to discover only the way to a world smelling unpleasantly of cabbage, watched over by a dirty old woman saying "Kwawk." Moreover, the lord of this underworld seems unimpressive: a big old man with a white beard sitting on a lavatory seat. Yet Javitt's words include many of Greene's own statements about the novelist's task. Like Greene, he looks at the familiar world with an unconventional eye. In addition, he and Maria are prototypes of Power, the supernatural or spiritual force whose loss from the modern world Greene has so frequently mourned.

He himself sought this ancient Power on his journey to "the heart of darkness" in 1934–35, when he followed the ancestral threads back to

Reprinted from "Greene's 'Under the Garden': Aesthetic Explorations," *Renascence* 17 (Summer 1965): 180–90, 194. Reprinted by permission of *Renascence*.

African "innocence." This was not a romantic journey, in spite of Greene's acknowledgement (in *In Search of a Character*) of Conrad's influence on his early work. He was not looking for the noble savage, but for the primitive, unspoiled vision: the purer pleasure and the purer terror of sharpened artistic sensibility. It was in Africa that Greene tried to discover "at what point we went astray." He emerged from his *Journey without Maps* to chart new fictional paths, beginning with *Brighton Rock*. Wilditch also "goes back"—first to the scene of his boyhood vacations, to a time before he had learned that "imagination was usually a quality to be suppressed." He too tries to discover a lost vision.

Wilditch's experience in rediscovering this lost childhood dream is a neat parable of Greene's artistic theory. Greene has written continually about the world of childhood, alluding to its cruelties and to its innocence again and again in his book reviews, novels, and film criticism. Metaphors drawn from his own schooldays recur in texts as varied as *The Heart of the Matter* and *Brighton Rock*. Repeatedly, Greene uses the phrase "lost childhood," an allusion identified in his volume of essays, where he quotes from AE's "Germinal":

> In ancient shadows and twilights
> Where childhood had strayed,
> The world's great sorrows were born
> And its heroes were made.
> In the lost boyhood of Judas
> Christ was betrayed.

It is worth noting that this poem opens with the line, "Call not the wanderer home as yet." Its final verse suggests: "Let thy young wanderer dream on: / Call him not home. / A door opens, a breath, a voice, / From the ancient room, / Speaks to him now . . ."

The ancient room to which Wilditch wanders in "Under the Garden" gives new depth to Greene's theme of the artist as wanderer, explorer, map-maker. He has said, "The explorer has the same creative sickness as the writer or the artist. . . . To fill in the map, as to fill in the characters or features of a human being, requires the urge to surrender and self-destruction." Although Greene writes, "It was plain that the young Wilditch's talents had not been for literature," the adult Wilditch is well aware that the author must "order and enrich the experience," and he examines that original experience, translating the childhood vision with the aid of his years of wandering in quest of Beauty.

The questing artist of Greene's creation is not simply a traveller and map-maker, however. He must look at the world with the eyes of childhood as well as the mind of maturity. Like the narrator of "The Innocent," working out and reinterpreting a childhood memory as he lay in bed beside a pickup, Lola, Wilditch revisits the scenes of innocence, remembering and re-forming the child's experience in order to reinterpret the present. In "The Innocent," the narrator recognized the distortions introduced by the cynicism of adult perception: the child's "uniquely beautiful" picture seemed momentarily more like an ugly drawing on a lavatory wall. Wilditch finds the meaning of *his* experience not in terms of a lavatory scrawl but in a tin chamberpot flecked with yellow paint. Even as he perceives its meaning, Wilditch recalls that the child found that "golden pot" uniquely beautiful, as beautiful as the drawing in "The Innocent."

Describing the early formative years of a writer, Greene has spoken of the "innocent eye dwelling frankly on a new unexplored world, the vistas of future experience at the end of the laurel walk." The vistas at the end of Wilditch's laurel walk eventually opened the way to his years of future experience travelling in search of Beauty (Javitt's daughter): "The purpose of life had suddenly come to me as it must have come to some future explorer when he noticed on a map for the first time an empty space in the heart of a continent."

Again, Wilditch's words clearly echo Greene's in *Journey without Maps*. Wilditch entering the heart of darkness below the tree resembles Greene, who described himself as "a complete amateur at travel in Africa . . . [with] no idea of what route to follow or the conditions he would meet." Greene even referred to his African journey as "a smash-and-grab raid into the primitive"—an amusing foreshadowing of Wilditch's experience with the treasure, which reminded him of the display in a jeweller's window. In spite of the finer artistic conscious-ness which Greene demonstrated after his journey, he was at first able only to see Africa in terms of such romantic adventures as *King Solomon's Mines*. The boy Wilditch also thought of "romantic explora-tions" and *Treasure Island* when he named the landmarks of his discovery. Yet the romantic storybook world does have something in common with actual exploration. Both belong to "the region of the imagination—the region of uncertainty, of not knowing the way about."

In the course of exploring the region of his own imagination, Greene found his way about four geographical areas that have come to serve as symbols in his artistic development. Liberia, Mexico, Indo-China, and the Congo in turn exposed new levels of artistic consciousness, which Greene expressed in psychological terminology. Liberia was the world of childhood "innocence," a beginning, "before we began to go wrong." Yet these children were in a "spiritual Limbo." He then went to Mexico, where he found "adolescent" violence that yet revealed a dramatic picture of secular power superseding religious glory and suggested "the appalling mysteries of love moving through a ravaged world." After his novels of love and hate, Greene travelled to Indo-China, where he discovered the representative adult of our "chromium-plated" civilization, that cliché-ridden "innocent" American Pyle, whose "writers and lecturers made a fool of him." But he also discovered that "Under the enormous shadow of the Cross it was better to be gay." After he had been suitably gay in his delightful self-mockeries *Loser Take All, The Complaisant Lover,* and *Our Man in Havana,* Greene went to the Congo "In Search of a Character." Here he finally identified the character of the adult Querry—perhaps his response to Camus' view of the Absurd Man as traveller, and certainly as artist returning to life (and death). Yet the "truth" which Greene says he sought on his journeys—one he defines as "a question of style" rather than any kind of philosophical probing—is also one of "eternal values," the religion of man's soul to God. Like T. S. Eliot, Greene sees in today's lost religious sense a loss to the world of fiction, a reduction of characters to "cardboard," without the "solidity and importance of men with souls to save or lose." Unlike Wilditch, who denies that he is religious, Greene admits of his own position. "Quand on est catholique, il ne faut pas chercher à faire du 'catholicisme.' Tout ce que l'on dit ou écrit respire inevitablement le catholicisme." [When one is a Catholic, it is not necessary to seek to be Catholic. Everything that one says or writes inevitably breathes Catholicism.]

Primarily, however, Wilditch expresses the problems of a writer. He learns the way to artistic truth. Entering an unknown region and determined to draw a map Wilditch, like his creator in this and many other seemingly deliberately teasing respects, is alternately attracted and repelled by the conditions of Javitt's world of mysterious Power, a world oddly touched by traces of civilization. Reading his boyhood story, a tale published six years after the original action, Wilditch is irritated by details he had omitted or altered. He wonders whether the boy had forgotten or was afraid to remember the actual experience (Greene has spoken of the novelist's need to "face his fears"). Yet Wilditch clings to the "fact" that he dreamed. Concluding, "A dream too was an experience," he begins to write an account of what he had found—or dreamed that he had found—when he first descended into the darkness under the garden.

In his essay, "Analysis of a Journey," later rephrased and incorporated into *Journey without Maps*, Greene spoke of the effect of Africa and its ancient Power upon the unconscious mind of the writer: "A quality of darkness was needed, of the inexplicable, something which has to be taken as a symbol because it has no obvious meaning for the conscious brain." He also quoted Kurt Heuser's *The Inner Journey*: "The interior: that might signify the heart of the continent, but also the heart of things, the mystery: and finally, the comprehension of himself in nature and in Time." That could be a description of Wilditch's journey, which continually echoes Greene's comparison of journey and dream. Wilditch says, recalling the details of his adventure, "Absolute reality belongs to dreams and not to life. . . . What seems is."

Wilditch travelled away from the "reality" of his mother's world, where the poetic imagination had always to be "rigidly controlled" and "speculation was discouraged." He found his own reality, as any writer must establish values for himself. His mother with her "very decided views" about any mysteries "wanted everything to be very clear." She could only tolerate "puzzles," the kind of mystery found in detective stories, where there is always an answer. But she could not approve the mysteries of imagination, of fairy stories, or of religious faith. When she wrote to the school about the "religious" feeling she was certain existed in her son's story, they responded with the comforting thought that his "little fantasy" was probably related to young Wilditch's school reading program, for the treasure of his story "is only too material, and quite at the mercy of those who break in and steal." His mother, a staunch Fabian (described in terms reminiscent of those used for Smythe in *The End of the Affair*), was not convinced; she retained a dislike for the laurel walk and the garden. Finally she hid the magazine containing the story, rather as the family for whom "God was taboo" tried to suppress the religious mystery of young James's experience in *The Potting Shed*. Yet—as this mystery was finally solved, or Sarah's hidden baptism became effective in *The End of the Affair*—the mystery of the garden could not be suppressed. Wilditch returned to the dark hidden room of his dream-reality, where the treasures of language and thought had not yet been contaminated by the clichés of popular culture or dulled by the stock responses typified in George Wilditch's lack of understanding.

George and his brother "seemed to be talking about different places and different people." George's unawareness of the hidden treasure beneath his garden is an extension of his refusal to take imaginative flight. He chides Wilditch for calling the pond a lake, for referring to "treasure" in an old quarry that actually contained only "iron stuff." Although he "had been in occupation" of the house for many years, George "had no idea of what might lie underneath the garden." It remained only a problem in taxation, management, and plumbing. For George is a member of the "chromium-plated" civilization of the west that Greene continually holds responsible for the clichés of popular entertainment.

Wilditch's flight from this stifling reality leads him into the realm of darkness, without maps, where he can discover the heart of things for himself. But the boundaries of dream and reality are as uncertain as the earlier geographical frontiers. We are never quite permitted to discover the source of Wilditch's story, in spite of Greene's careful separation of adult re-creation and childhood vision by shifting from a third-person narrative to Wilditch's. For even as Artist-Wilditch separates his "corrected" version from the schoolboy fiction, he continually comments on the impossibility of separating dream from life. "A dream can only contain what one has experienced, or, if you have sufficient faith in Jung, what our ancestors have experienced." Yet even as he "explains" the story, Wilditch observes that it is no more than a pale imitation of the original action. He doubts that the boy could have been aware of the "simple facts" which keep bringing his dark experience "back to ordinary life." He cannot decide, however, whether he is dealing with child's invention, with "real" adventure, or with experiences that have "accumulated like coral around the original dream."

Thus Wilditch's story becomes an exercise in creative map-making for the reader. As Greene has said in another context, "The writer's task is the correct setting of a question." The writer must stimulate the reader to wonder, and to choose. He must create a world of sympathy (for "gray and black characters alike"); communicate a mood or atmosphere, as Wilditch communicates the cabbage odor and the strange routine of the dank underground passage; suggest moral values without ever sinking to pious homily, as Javitt's pronouncements demand re-weighing of conventional commandments. He must avoid senti-mentality—hence the detachment of Wilditch's viewpoint, the repeated reminders of his "story," and the attempts to separate the primary reaction from the later judgment and rewriting of experience.

Thus the map metaphor is an appropriate symbolization of the artistic vision confronting the world that has been labelled (unsatisfactorily) by others, by men using the dead language of convention. By walking each path for himself, as Greene walked through Africa, and as Wilditch crawls and walks through the world below the familiar garden, the writer examines experience at first hand instead of accepting such clichés as Ida's identification of "right" and "wrong" in *Brighton Rock* or the confusion of "love" and "hate" in Bendrix's interpretation of *The End of the Affair*. Too often, as Greene observes, the popular novelist substitutes sentimental clichés and distorting commonplaces for "life as it is and life as it ought to be."

Arthur Rowe in *The Ministry of Fear* also found himself through experiences in a garden, although he too first had "the wrong map." Like Rowe, and like the psychoanalyst of Greene's early essay, Wilditch pieces together the fragments of the past, examining these fragments in a manner that suggests the epigraph of *Journey without Maps*: "The life of an individual is in many respects like a child's dissected map. If I could live a hundred years . . . I could put the pieces together until they made a properly connected whole." Faced with death, and the vague consolation that "there's always hope," Wilditch seeks the fragments from the past of his dissected life while he attempts to answer his question.

Wilditch's question is the decision, "Whether I want my particular kind of life prolonged." He adds that he isn't a religious man and that he has "no curiosity at all about the future." He also knows that the past is "different." About the Dark Backward he is endlessly curious, although he compares himself to a Civil War leader mortally wounded and attempting to rid himself of illusions by "seeing them again with clear and moribund eyes, so that he might be quite bankrupt when death came." Instead of bankruptcy, however, he discovers the richness of restored perception: "Curiosity was growing inside him like the cancer." The artist is alive again, as Querry was, and like Querry Wilditch is faced with death. Nevertheless, there *is* hope, for—again as in *A Burnt-Out Case*—"The man who starts looking for God has already found Him."

Wilditch's creator is Catholic and the religious overtones of the story cannot be denied. But the story is not a narrowly religious parable. Christ's injunction to the sinner wishing to enter God's kingdom to become a child, is also advice on the craft of friction, expressed through Greene's familiar theme of "lost childhood." Greene has repeatedly praised the "admirable objectivity" of childhood—the time when we are not yet conditioned by other people's judgments. Childhood is a time of "virgin sensibility," and as Greene notes in "Herbert Read," the creative spirit is tied to innocence, the "stock of innocence" is essential for a writer. This unspoiled quality is quite different from that false innocence of Pyle, whose "writers and lecturers made a fool of him" in *The Quiet American.* "The undimmed window of the innocent eye" is the child's eye; but as noted above, in "The Innocent" Greene shows that the eye can only perceive the truth when it has an adult's powers of judgment.

Greene discovered the significance of "childhood innocence" in 1935, during his journey into the heart of darkness. Returning to England, he heard its loss symbolized in the cry of a tenement child—a symbol made flesh in the ensuing entertainment and novel: Raven in *This Gun for Hire* and Pinkie in *Brighton Rock.* Wilditch returns to the innocent dream of childhood, journeying back in time and in memory (again like the narrator of "The Innocent"), in order to re-create the myth, to restore the dulled imagination, to purge the crippling effects of his mother's response to the boy's fictional imitation of a dream action. He discovers the purpose of life, the significance of his lifelong quest, by following the dark threads of memory deep underground.

Such a dark place frequently offers enlightenment in Greene's work. The enlightenment may be religious—as in *The Power and the Glory*, where the dark prison cell brings to the whisky priest an awareness of "the convincing mystery—that we were made in God's image." Yet Greene's use of "the heart of darkness" and "the heart of the matter" is usually no more than "the hint of an explanation," phrases combined in *The Heart of the Matter* to describe the forty-day survival ordeal of a child in an open boat. Greene writes of another mystery: "J'ai toujours été préoccupé par le mystère du peché, il a toujours été à la base de mes livres." [I have always been preoccupied by the mystery of sin, it has always been at the base of my books.] Neither God nor sinner can claim exclusive rights to this dark center, however. Like Bendrix's discovery, it may be the transformation of hate into love; or like Wilditch's, the discovery of the existence of Beauty.

"Beauty" sprung from a one-legged old man on a lavatory seat and a dumb hag in faded blue and sequins is as ambiguous a term as others in Greene's fiction. The questions raised by Greene's use of such labels as "justice" in *It's a Battlefield*, "belief" in *The Third Man*, "faith" in "A Visit to Morin," or "love" in *The End of the Affair*, are asked again by Javitt. Javitt's use of language stresses the need for new words and different meanings. Not only do his riddles challenge young Wilditch. He also takes such familiar terms as "white elephant stall" at a garden fête and converts the words to "royal beasts" and man's fate—word-play that is perhaps symbolic of the linguistic traps awaiting writers. In Javitt's world, Time has "a different meaning"; the world's time is unrelated to that of the dark underground, and the ruins of time become transformed into phallic pillars. Javitt challenges Wilditch's conventional use of language with practical, cryptic, and even poetic comment, although the boy does not immediately understand. This advice is "stored in [Wilditch's] memory like a code uncracked which waits for a clue or an inspiration." Javitt, the dirty old man on a lavatory seat, is the New Muse.

Behind this role lies Javitt's resemblance to the ancient Power, which might be loosely identified with the creative force. He is also clearly associated with concepts of godhead, in spite of Wilditch's observation that Javitt resembles Darwin's carrier pigeon (reminiscent of Greene's opinion of "Darwinian materialism"). Like the Hebrew Yahweh, he has another name: one too sacred to be spoken. His symbolic value is continually hinted, whether in his knowledge of "the first name of all," his resemblance to a crucifix, or his promise of forgiveness "seventy times seven." Lest we are tempted to confuse Javitt with God Himself, however, we are told of his resemblance to an old tree-trunk, thus setting him back in the fictional world of *A Burnt-Out Case* by means of the implied resemblance to the natural man, Deo Gratias, the leper who helped to restore the dulled perceptions of the artist Querry.

Javitt challenges the boy, "Haven't I given you a kingdom here of all the treasures of the earth and all the fruits of it"—an echo of the King in Querry's parable. He adds, "You go and defy me with a spoon laid the wrong way," hinting again at the obedience demanded by God, an obedience not always understood by the suffering Catholic heroes of Greene's fiction. Wilditch writes: "For all [Javitt's] freedom of speech and range of thought, I found there were tiny rules which had to be obeyed." That these rules include the method of folding a newspaper and the placement of a spoon should not preclude their serious interpretation.

On the other hand, the satirical hints of these rules, of the golden po's "sacramental" quality, of Javitt finding portents in tea leaves, should not be taken as evidence that Greene has begun to satirize religious belief or that he is mocking the spiritual dimension of his fictional world. "Under the enormous shadow of the Cross it is better to be gay."

The parable of the Jeweller in *A Burnt-Out Case* described an artist whose treasure had been reduced from great cathedrals to golden letters of Marque. But the treasure in "Under the Garden," in spite of the adult Wilditch's "skepticism of middle-age"—the comparison of the jewels with the artificial display of a cheap store window—is a symbol of promise. It would, however, be a mistake to limit the treasure to religious meaning, in spite of its setting in an egg-shaped hall, where the swinging lamp resembles a censer, Javitt makes ceremonial preparations, and Maria dons a hat. And to dismiss these or the "sacramental" golden po as Greenean whimsy, as further examples of his too-rarely recognized sense of humor, is no more satisfactory than to read them as a religious riddle. Taken as symbols of artistic quest and discovery, however, they do contribute a number of footnotes to Greene's literary intentions. Javitt chides the boy: "You think you can just take a peek . . . and go away." This suggests a criticism of the superficial writer. It is also a precise description of the attitude of so many of Greene's critics. In the interview "Propos de table avec Graham Greene" he observed: "Quant aux incroyants, ils ne sont pas scandalisés, mais montrent une incompréhension presque totale, même les critique les plus intelligents. Ils sont si loin de toute vue chrétienne de l'homme qu'ils ne peuvent entrer dans mon univers." [As to the unbelievers, they are not scandalized, but show an almost total incomprehension, even the most intelligent critics. They are so far removed from a Christian view of mankind that they are unable to enter into my universe.] These critics and other writers should not be content to just "take a peek" at the varying worlds created by questing authors. Critic and reader must enter into the fictional world, encouraged by the creation of a writer who has carefully explored the mapless paths of the world about him and faced its flaws and inconsistencies, what Greene calls the "gray and black" of our existence.

The keeper of the key to Javitt's treasure, the literary inspiration, is Maria. She is Woman—"sister, wife, mother, daughter. . . . What difference does it make?" Her name places her in the complex family of Greene's recurrent character, Anne-Marie. (It is worth noting that three Christian names: Mary, Virgin or Magdaline; Anne, mother of Mary; and Rose, symbol of Christ's pain; are frequently at the center of Greene's novels.) Her appearance suggests the mysterious Power, the power Greene felt in Africa and recalled in terms of a witch that haunted his childhood. Like the witch-voiced Mrs. Baines in "The Basement Room" and the dark devils of Greene's African villages, Maria inspires fear in Wilditch. Yet it is her force which ultimately propels him back into the real world. She forces Wilditch back to the world where he must interpret the clues provided by the oracular Javitt.

Javitt's riddles provoke thought; Maria's actions rouse primitive instincts. Once again, Greene hints at the dual nature of the artist's inspiration. This duality is further stressed in what Wilditch calls "a strange balance"—the continual tension between fear and happiness or laughter. Most important, however, is Javitt's admonition: "Be disloyal. It's your duty to the human race. . . . Be a double agent—and never let either of the two sides know your real name. The same applies to women and God. They both respect a man they don't own, and they'll go on raising the price they are willing to offer. Didn't Christ say that very thing. . . . The obedient flock didn't give the shepherd any satisfaction or the loyal son interest his father."

In spite of Greene's identification as a "Catholic" author, it is the first part of Javitt's advice that he regards as most important. When Javitt says, "Be disloyal," he might be Greene himself sending a potential writer out into the world. In *Why Do I Write?* Greene had said that belonging to the Catholic Church would present him with grave problems as a writer if he were not "saved by my disloyalty. . . . Literature presents a personal moral, and the personal morality of an individual is seldom identical with the morality of the group to which he belongs." In a second letter of this exchange of views between Greene, Elisabeth Bowen, and V. S. Pritchett, he repeated his emphasis on the "importance and the virtue of disloyalty," claiming that disloyalty encourages the writer to "roam experimentally through any human mind: it gives to the novelist the extra dimension of sympathy"—the ability to communicate a sympathetic comprehension of good and evil characters living in this world. Greene again stressed that the writer should be disloyal to the emotional and ideological clichés of his time, in order to avoid writing the sort of popular novel that substitutes cliché for truth.

Yet whatever fancies Javitt encourages in the boy, Wilditch notes that the old adventure-dream always "kept coming back to ordinary life with simple facts." As in Greene's own works, the story should keep its characters in *this* world, its narrative set in the actual world, its plot related to "the way men really act," instead of being confined to the individual waves—the thoughts and fantasies of the cardboard characters Greene has so often attacked.

Javitt is not a sentimentalist. Whether he is discussing beauty or sex, monkeys or women, his conversation with Wilditch suggests the kind of author-reader dialogue which Greene so admires. Instead of sentimentalized sex and violence, the tired phrases of popular "entertainment," Javitt offers Beauty spawned by Maria in the dark room and the monkeys' view of death as an "accident." When he tells Wilditch, "Forget your mother and your father too," or "Forget all your schoolmasters teach you," he is again urging the fresh vision, the "disloyalty" of Greene's own creations.

There are, of course, hints of theological interpretation in Javitt's advice. The liturgical elements already noted, whether of Catholic ceremony or Christian symbol, are bound to remind any Greene reader of similar phrasing in his novels and stories. Although the experience was scarcely a religious one to the small boy, his mother had feared the worst, and the reawakened Wilditch, faced with the reality of his gold-flecked po, notes "She had reason to fear." For the whole context of this "dark mystery" is drawn from religious dialectic.

Like Javitt, Wilditch occasionally speaks with Greene's own voice, or assumes his creator's familiar mannerisms. His brother describes Wilditch as a "restless man," and adds terms reminiscent of Greene's allusions to his own restlessness and need to travel. Wilditch's curiosity about the world of darkness under the tree echoes Greene's own interest in Africa's creative heart of darkness. When Wilditch hears of Beauty he becomes like an explorer noticing a blank place on the map. When he finally becomes "achingly tired as though at the end of a long journey," he repeats Greene's experiences in *Journey without Maps*, an idea recurring in contexts as varied as *The Lawless Roads*, *The Man Within*, and *Our Man in Havana*.

The story suggests a myth through which Greene can express his preoccupation with the mystery of Faith, the difficulties of belief, the loss of "mystique" from today's religious life. It is difficult to avoid the suspicion that Greene's myth refers, at least obliquely, to Jung's opinion of religious failure in the West, the vision of God's underground counterpart, the nameless subterranean God. Javitt, "less interested in conversation than in the recital of some articles of belief," is indeed the ancient oracle, the guardian of the treasure. Appropriately, the jewels are hidden—even the boy must wait for the privilege of revelation—for as Greene had written thirty years before in *Stamboul Train*: "We have been for a thousand years in the wilderness of a Christian world, where only the secret treasure was safe." For the author, the religious sense is important in terms of his craft. Though he does not share Jung's confidence in fantasy as a successor to Christian Faith, his personal faith is something different. The "air" of Catholicism inseparable from Greene's work or the "disloyalty" he advocates carry equal weight in the ultimate fiction, so long as the awareness of Good and Evil is there. Wilditch's growing curiosity may be a question of fiction or of faith, but it comes only after experience. His imaginative encounter with the jewels and the sources of language sends him in search of Beauty. Yet "it was only years later, after a deal of literature and learning and knowledge at second hand" that he could record a "true" version of his story. He could not remain in the underground world of darkness and sequins, canned sardines and cabbage broth, lavatory seats and old newspapers. Although his first glimpse of the treasure had made him feel that he must give up "all the riches of the world, its pursuits and enjoyments," he had to return to "the world he knew." In that world he could record for the dull George and the faithless Mother the world of mystery and imagination "Under the Garden."

Chronology

<table>
<tr><td>1904</td><td>Graham Greene born 2 October in Berkhamsted, England.</td></tr>
<tr><td>1912</td><td>Enrolled in Berkhamsted School, where his father is headmaster.</td></tr>
<tr><td>1921</td><td>Psychoanalyzed by Kenneth Richmond.</td></tr>
<tr><td>1922–1925</td><td>Attends Balliol College, Oxford; edits Oxford Outlook.</td></tr>
<tr><td>1925</td><td>Babbling April (poems).</td></tr>
<tr><td>1926</td><td>Works for the Nottingham Journal without salary; converts to Roman Catholicism; starts working for the London Times.</td></tr>
<tr><td>1927</td><td>Marries Vivien Dayrell-Browning.</td></tr>
<tr><td>1929</td><td>The Man Within (first published novel).</td></tr>
<tr><td>1930</td><td>The Name of Action (novel).</td></tr>
<tr><td>1931</td><td>Rumour at Nightfall (novel), later withdrawn.</td></tr>
<tr><td>1932</td><td>Stamboul Train (novel, entitled Orient Express in the United States).</td></tr>
<tr><td>1933</td><td>Daughter, Lucy Caroline, born 28 December.</td></tr>
<tr><td>1934</td><td>It's a Battlefield (novel); travels to Liberia.</td></tr>
<tr><td>1935</td><td>The Basement Room (first collection of short stories); The Bear Fell Free (short story); England Made Me (novel, entitled The Shipwrecked in the United States).</td></tr>
<tr><td>1935–1939</td><td>Film critic for the Spectator.</td></tr>
<tr><td>1936</td><td>A Gun for Sale (novel, entitled This Gun for Hire in the United States); Journey without Maps (an account of his trip to Liberia); son, Francis, born 13 September.</td></tr>
<tr><td>1937</td><td>Assists in the editing of the magazine Night and Day.</td></tr>
<tr><td>1938</td><td>Brighton Rock (novel); travels to Mexico to report on the persecution of the Catholic church in Tobasco and Chiapas.</td></tr>
</table>

1939   *The Lawless Roads* (an account of his trip to Mexico, entitled *Another Mexico* in the United States); *The Confidential Agent* (novel).

1940   *The Power and the Glory* (novel, entitled *The Labyrinthine Ways* in the United States); begins working for the Ministry of Information.

1941   Becomes literary editor and drama critic for the *Spectator;* starts working for the Foreign Office in Africa and England.

1943   *The Ministry of Fear* (novel).

1944   Appointed director of Eyre and Spottiswoode, publishers.

1945   Writes book reviews for the *Evening Standard.*

1947   *Nineteen Stories.*

1948   *The Heart of the Matter* (novel).

1950   *The Third Man* (novel).

1951   *The End of the Affair* (novel); *The Lost Childhood and Other Essays*; travels to Malaya and Indochina.

1952   Receives Catholic Literary Award for *The End of the Affair.*

1953   *The Living Room* (his first play) published; the play is produced in London at Wyndham's Theatre on 16 April; travels to Kenya for the *Sunday Times.*

1954   *Twenty-One Stories* (a revision of *Nineteen Stories*); travels to Indochina as a correspondent for the *Sunday Times* and *Figaro.*

1955   *The Quiet American* (novel); *Loser Takes All* (novel); travels to Indochina and Poland for the *Sunday Times* and *Figaro.*

1956   Travels to Haiti.

1957   *The Potting Shed* (drama) is published in the United States; the play is produced in New York at the Bijou Theater on 29 January; travels to Cuba, China, and the Soviet Union.

1958   *Our Man in Havana* (novel); *The Potting Shed* is published in England and produced in London at the Globe Theatre on 5 February; appointed director of the Bodley Head, publishers.

1959   *The Complaisant Lover* (drama); the play is produced in

London by Sir John Gielgud at the Globe Theatre on 18 June; travels to the Belgian Congo.

1961 *A Burnt-Out Case* (novel); *In Search of a Character* (an account of his African travels); *The Complaisant Lover* is produced in New York at the Ethel Barrymore Theater on 1 November.

1962 Receives Honorary Doctor of Letters degree, Cambridge University.

1963 *A Sense of Reality* (short stories); travels to Haiti for the *Sunday Telegraph*.

1964 *Carving a Statue* (drama); the play is produced in London at the Haymarket Theatre on 17 September.

1966 *The Comedians* (novel); separates from his wife and leaves England to establish permanent residence in Antibes, a small seaport town on the French Riviera.

1967 *May We Borrow your Husband? and Other Comedies of the Sexual Life* (short stories); travels to Sierra Leone for the *Observer*.

1969 *Collected Essays*; *Travels with My Aunt* (novel); travels to Argentina and Paraguay for the *Sunday Telegraph*.

1971 *A Sort of Life* (autobiography); returns to Argentina.

1972 *Collected Stories*; *The Pleasure Dome* (collected film criticism).

1973 *The Honorary Consul* (novel).

1974 *Lord Rochester's Monkey* (biography of John Wilmot, earl of Rochester).

1975 *The Return of A. J. Raffles* (drama).

1978 *The Human Factor* (novel).

1980 *Ways of Escape* (autobiography); *Doctor Fischer of Geneva or the Bomb Party* (novel).

1982 *Monsignor Quixote* (novel); *J'Accuse* (a pamphlet in which Greene attacks corrupt government officials of the French Riviera).

1984 *Getting to Know the General: The Story of an Involvement* (an account of Greene's friendship with General Omar Torrijos Herrera).

1985   *The Tenth Man* (novel).

1988   *The Captain and the Enemy* (novel).

1990   *The Last Word* (short stories).

1991   Dies 3 April, at La Providence Hospital, in Vevey, near Lake Geneva, Switzerland, of a blood disease.

Selected Bibliography

Primary Works

(Listed in chronological order)

Collections of Short Fiction

The Basement Room. London: Cresset Press, 1935. Includes "The Basement Room," "The End of the Party," "I Spy," "Brother," "Jubilee," "A Chance for Mr. Lever," "Proof Positive," and "A Day Saved."

The Bear Fell Free. London: Grayson and Grayson, 1935.

Nineteen Stories. London: Heinemann, 1947. Reprints all of the stories from *The Basement Room* and adds 11 more: "The Innocent," "A Drive in the Country," "Across the Bridge," "The Lottery Ticket," "The Second Death," "A Little Place off the Edgeware Road," "The Case for the Defence," "When Greek Meets Greek," "Men at Work," "Alas, Poor Maling," and "The Other Side of the Border." The American edition, published by Viking in 1949, replaces "The Lottery Ticket" with "The Hint of an Explanation," a story that appeared in 1948, a year after the publication of the British collection.

Twenty-One Stories. London: Heinemann, 1954. Reprints 17 of the stories in *Nineteen Stories*, omitting "The Lottery Ticket" and "The Other Side of the Border," and adding "The Hint of an Explanation," "The Blue Film," "Special Duties," and "The Destructors." The American edition, published by Viking, omits "The Other Side of the Border," and adds "The Blue Film," "Special Duties," and "The Destructors."

A Sense of Reality. London: Bodley Head, 1963. Includes "Under the Garden," "A Visit to Morin," "Dream of a Strange Land," and "A Discovery in the Woods."

May We Borrow Your Husband? and Other Comedies of the Sexual Life. London: Bodley Head, 1967. Includes "May We Borrow Your Husband?," "A Shocking Accident," "Awful When You Think of It," "Beauty," "Mortmain," "The Root of All Evil," "Cheap in August," "Doctor Crombie," "The Over-Night Bag," "The Invisible Japanese Gentlemen," "Chagrin in Three Parts," and "Two Gentle People."

Collected Stories. London: Bodley Head/William Heinemann, 1972. Appears simply to reprint the three previous collections (*Twenty-One Stories, A Sense*

153

of Reality, and *May We Borrow Your Husband?*), but Greene has added three previously uncollected stories to *A Sense of Reality*: "The Church Militant" (1956), "Dear Dr. Falkenheim" (1963), and "The Blessing" (1966). An oddity of the *Collected Edition* is that it arranges the three previous collections in reverse chronological order.

The Last Word and Other Stories. London: Reinhardt, 1990. Includes "The Last Word," "The Moment of Truth," "An Old Man's Memory," "A Branch of the Service," "An Appointment with the General," "The Man Who Stole the Eiffel Tower," "Work Not in Progress," "The Lieutenant Died Last," "The News in English," "The Lottery Ticket," "Murder for the Wrong Reason," and "The New House."

Uncollected Short Fiction in Periodicals

"The Tick of the Clock." *Berkhamstedian* 40 (December 1920): 118–19.
"The Poetry of Modern Life." *Berkhamstedian* 41 (March 1921): 3–4.
"Castles in the Air." *Berkhamstedian* 41 (December 1921) 111–13.
"The Creation of Beauty," place of publication unknown.
"The Tyranny of Realism." *Berkhamstedian* 42 (March 1922): 2–3.
"Magic." *Weekly Westminster Gazette* 1 (6 May 1922): 16.
"The Trial of Pan." *Oxford Outlook* 5 (February 1923): 47–50.
"The Improbable Tale of the Archbishop of Canterbridge." *Cherwell*, n.s., 12 (15 November 1924): 187, 189, 191.
"The Lord Knows." *Oxford Chronicle*, 5 June 1925, p. 116.
"Voyage in the Dark." *Spectator* 161 (16 September 1938): 437.
"The Escapist." *Spectator* 162 (13 January 1939): 48–49.
"All But Empty." *Strand Magazine* 112 (March 1947): 66–69.

Novels

The Man Within. London: Heinemann, 1929.
The Name of Action. London: Heinemann, 1930.
Rumour at Nightfall. London: Heinemann, 1931.
Stamboul Train. London: Heinemann, 1932.
It's a Battlefield. London: Heinemann, 1934.
England Made Me. London: Heinemann, 1935.
A Gun for Sale. London: Heinemann, 1936.
Brighton Rock. London: Heinemann, 1938.
The Confidential Agent. London: Heinemann, 1939.
The Power and the Glory. London: Heinemann, 1940.
The Ministry of Fear. London: Heinemann, 1943.
The Heart of the Matter. London: Heinemann, 1948.
The Third Man. London: Heinemann, 1950.

The End of the Affair. London: Heinemann, 1951.
Loser Takes All. London: Heinemann, 1955.
The Quiet American. London: Heinemann, 1955.
Our Man in Havana. London: Heinemann, 1958.
A Burnt-Out Case. London: Heinemann, 1961.
The Comedians. London: Bodley Head, 1966.
Travels with My Aunt. London: Bodley Head, 1969.
The Honorary Consul. London: Bodley Head, 1973.
The Human Factor. London: Bodley Head, 1978.
Doctor Fischer of Geneva or the Bomb Party. London: Bodley Head, 1980.
Monsignor Quixote. London: Bodley Head, 1982.
The Tenth Man. London: Bodley Head, 1985.
The Captain and the Enemy. London: Bodley Head, 1988.

Other Writings

Babbling April. Oxford: Basil Blackwell, 1925. (Poems)
Journey without Maps: A Travel Book. London: Heinemann, 1936. (An account of his travels through Liberia)
The Lawless Roads. London: Longmans, 1939. (An account of his travels in Mexico)
The Lost Childhood and Other Essays. London: Eyre and Spottiswoode, 1951.
The Living Room. London: Heinemann, 1953. (Drama)
The Potting Shed. London: Heinemann, 1958. (Drama)
The Complaisant Lover. London: Heinemann, 1959. (Drama)
In Search of a Character: Two African Journals. London: Bodley Head, 1961.
Carving a Statue. London: Bodley Head, 1964. (Drama)
Collected Essays. London: Bodley Head, 1969.
A Sort of Life. London: Bodley Head, 1971. (Autobiography)
The Pleasure Dome: Collected Film Criticism, 1935–1940. Edited by John Russell-Taylor. London: Secker and Warburg, 1972.
Lord Rochester's Monkey. London: Bodley Head, 1974. (Biography of John Wilmot, earl of Rochester)
An Impossible Woman: The Memories of Dottoressa Moor of Capri. London: Bodley Head, 1975. (An edition of Moor's memoirs)
Ways of Escape. London: Bodley Head, 1980. (Autobiography)
The Great Jowett. London: Bodley Head, 1981. (Radio drama, first aired on BBC in 1939)
J'Accuse: The Dark Side of Nice. London: Bodley Head, 1982. (Exposé)
Yes and No and *For Whom the Bell Chimes.* London: Bodley Head, 1983. (Drama)
Getting to Know the General. London: Bodley Head, 1984. (An account of his friendship with General Omar Torrijos Herrera, president of Panama)

Selected Bibliography

Graham Greene. Edited by Judith Adamson. New York: Viking, 1991. (Collection of essays, reviews, and travel pieces)

Secondary Works

Biographies

Sherry, Norman. *The Life of Graham Greene*. Vol. 1, 1904–1939. New York: Viking, 1989–. A projected two-volume work.

Critical Monographs

Adamson, Judith. *Graham Greene and Cinema*. Norman, Okla.: Pilgrim Books, 1984.
Allot, Kenneth, and Miriam Farris. *The Art of Graham Greene*. London: Hamish Hamilton, 1951.
Atkins, John. *Graham Greene: A Biographical and Literary Study*. London: Calder and Boyars, 1966.
Boardman, Gwenn R. *Graham Greene: The Aesthetics of Exploration*. Gainesville: University of Florida Press, 1971.
Couto, Maria. *Graham Greene: On the Frontier*. London: Macmillan, 1988.
DeVitis, A. A. *Graham Greene*. Boston: Twayne, 1986.
Erdinast-Vulcan, Daphna. *Graham Greene's Childless Fathers*. New York: St. Martin's Press, 1988.
Evans, R. O., ed. *Graham Greene: Some Critical Considerations*. Lexington: University of Kentucky Press, 1963.
Falk, Quentin. *Travels in Greeneland: The Cinema of Graham Greene*. London: Quartet Books, 1984.
Hynes, Samuel L., ed. *Graham Greene: A Collection of Critical Essays*. Englewood Cliffs, N.J.: Prentice-Hall, 1973.
Kelly, Richard. *Graham Greene*. New York: Ungar, 1984.
Kunkel, Francis L. *The Labyrinthine Ways of Graham Greene*. New York: Sheed and Ward, 1960.
Mesnet, Marie-Beatrice. *Graham Greene and the Heart of the Matter*. London: Cresset Press, 1954.
Meyers, Jeffrey, ed. *Graham Greene: A Revaluation*. London: Macmillan, 1990.
O'Prey, Paul. *A Reader's Guide to Graham Greene*. Worcester: Thames and Hudson, 1988.
Phillips, Gene D. *Graham Greene: The Films of His Fiction*. New York: Teachers College Press, 1974.
Pryce-Jones, David. *Graham Greene*. Edinburgh: Oliver and Boyd, 1963.
Sharrock, Roger. *Saints, Sinners, and Comedians: The Novels of Graham Greene*.

Turnbridge Wells, England, and Notre Dame, Ind.: Burns and Oates/ University of Notre Dame Press, 1984.

Spurling, John. *Graham Greene.* London: Methuen, 1983.

Thomas, Brian. *An Underground Fate: The Idiom of Romance in the Later Novels of Graham Greene.* Athens: University of Georgia Press, 1988.

Wolfe, Peter. *Graham Greene the Entertainer.* Carbondale: Southern Illinois University Press, 1972.

————., ed. *Essays in Graham Greene, an Annual Review.* Greenwood, Fla.: Penkevill, 1987.

Critical Essays

Boardman, Gwenn R. "Greene's 'Under the Garden': Aesthetic Explorations." *Renascence* 17 (Summer 1965): 180–90, 194.

Coulthard, A. R. "Graham Greene's 'The Hint of an Explanation': A Reinterpretation." *Studies in Short Fiction* 8 (Fall 1971): 601–5.

Duran, Leopoldo. "The Hint of an Explanation of Graham Greene." *Contemporary Review* 226 (March 1975): 152–55.

Lerner, Laurence. "Graham Greene." *Critical Quarterly* 5 (Autumn 1963): 217–31.

Liberman, M. M. "The Uses of Anti-Fiction: Greene's 'Across the Bridge.'" *Georgia Review* 27 (1973): 321–28.

McDougal, Stuart Y. "Visual Tropes: An Analysis of *The Fallen Idol.*" *Style* 9 (Fall 1975): 502–13.

O'Faoláin, Sean. "Graham Greene: I Suffer, Therefore I Am." In his *The Vanishing Hero: Studies in the Novelists of the Twenties*, 45–72. Boston: Little, Brown, 1956.

Ower, John. "Dark Parable: History and Theology in Graham Greene's 'The Destructors.'" *Cithara* (November 1975): 69–78.

Taylor, Marion A., and John Clark. "Further Sources for 'The Second Death' by Graham Greene." *Papers on English Language and Literature* 1 (Autumn 1965): 378–80.

Wassmer, Thomas A., S.J., "Faith and Belief: A Footnote to Greene's 'Visit to Morin.'" *Renascence* 11 (1959): 84–88.

Wobbe, Roland A. "Tyranny's Triangle: Patterns in Greene's Juvenilia and Major Works." *College Literature* 12 (1985): 1–10.

Zabel, Morton Dauwen. "Graham Greene: The Best and the Worst." In his *Craft and Character in Modern Fiction*, 276–96. New York: Viking Press, 1957.

Zambrano, Ana Laura. "Greene's Visions of Childhood: 'The Basement Room' and *The Fallen Idol.*" *Literature and Film Quarterly* 2 (Fall 1974): 324–31.

Selected Bibliography

Interviews and Letters

Allain, Marie-Françoise. *The Other Man: Conversations with Graham Greene.* London: Bodley Head, 1983.

Why Do I Write? London: Percival Marshall, 1948. (An exchange of views expressed in letters between Graham Greene, Elizabeth Bowen, and V. S. Pritchett)

Bibliographies

Birmingham, William. "Graham Greene Criticism: A Bibliographical Study." *Thought* 27 (Spring 1952): 72–100.

Cassis, A. F. *Graham Greene: An Annotated Bibliography of Criticism.* Metuchen, N.J.: Scarecrow, 1981.

Wobbe, Roland A. *Graham Greene: A Bibliography and Guide to Research.* New York: Garland, 1979.

Index

Index

Index

Maupassant, Guy de, 98, 105
Mauriac, François, 47, 109, 114
Mexico, 28–29, 70, 73–75, 92–94
Ministry of Information, 33–34

Nazism, 125, 126
New Statesman, 51
News Chronicle, 23
Nichols, Anthony, 62
Nietzsche, Friedrich, 126
Norris, Lewis: *Epic of Hades*, 15

O'Faoláin, Sean, 88
Orwell, George, 84
Oxford Chronicle, 14
Oxford Outlook, 11, 14

Potter, Beatrix, 10
Pound, Ezra, 115
Pritchett, V. S., 98, 105, 145
Punch, 53, 78, 79

Reade, Charles, 115
Richmond, Kenneth, 4, 7, 11, 51
Robb, Brian, 95
Rochester, John Wilmot, earl of, 54, 55, 56
Rushdie, Salman, 86

Scott, Captain Robert F., 6
"Shades of Greene," 97
Shelley, Percy Bysshe, 11
Sherry, Norman, 4, 6, 15, 28, 38
Sklare, Arnold B., 121, 123
Smart, Christopher, 115
Spectator, 93, 94
Stevenson, Robert Louis, 30, 137
Strand Magazine, 73, 76, 95
stream of consciousness, 89, 98
Swinburne, Algernon, 11

Thatcher, Margaret, 86, 87
Thomas, Brian, 42, 49
Thomson, James: "The Seasons," 59
Tolstoy, Leo, 116
Torrijos, General Omar, 79–81
Turgenev, Ivan, 116

Weekly Westminster Gazette, 10
Wheeler, A. H., 3–4, 15
Wobbe, Roland, 8, 9, 15
Wordsworth, William, 3, 4, 28, 42
Wren, Christopher, 126

Yeats, William Butler, 45, 54, 126
Yonge, Charlotte: *The Little Duke*, 10

The Author

Richard Kelly is Lindsay Young Professor of English at the University of Tennessee, Knoxville. He is the author of *The Best of Mr. Punch: The Humorous Writings of Douglas Jerrold* (1970), *Douglas Jerrold* (1972), *The Andy Griffith Show* (1981/1985), *George du Maurier* (1983), *Graham Greene* (1984), *Daphne du Maurier* (1987), *V. S. Naipaul* (1989), and *Lewis Carroll* (1990). His essays on nineteenth- and twentieth-century British literature have appeared in *College Literature, University of Toronto Quarterly, Studies in English Literature, Studies in Browning, Studies in Short Fiction, Victorian Poetry, Victorian Newsletter,* and the [London] *Independent.* He is currently completing a book about the North Carolina watermen.

The Editor

General Editor Gordon Weaver earned his B.A. in English at the University of Wisconsin-Milwaukee in 1961; his M.A. in English at the University of Illinois, where he studied as a Woodrow Wilson Fellow, in 1962; and his Ph.D. in English and creative writing at the University of Denver in 1970. He is author of several novels, including *Count a Lonely Cadence, Give Him a Stone, Circling Byzantium,* and most recently *The Eight Corners of the World* (1988). Many of his numerous short stories are collected in *The Entombed Man of Thule, Such Waltzing Was Not Easy, Getting Serious, Morality Play, A World Quite Round,* and *Men Who Would Be Good* (1991). Recognition of his fiction includes the St. Lawrence Award for Fiction (1973), two National Endowment for the Arts Fellowships (1974, 1989), and the O. Henry First Prize (1979). He edited *The American Short Story, 1945–1980: A Critical History,* and is currently editor of *Cimarron Review.* He is professor of English at Oklahoma State University and serves as an adjunct member of the faculty of the Vermont College Master of Fine Arts in Writing Program. Married, and the father of three daughters, he lives in Stillwater, Oklahoma.